DAILY
DECREES

for Family Blessing *and* Breakthrough

Defeat the Assignments of Hell Against Your Family
and Create Heavenly Atmospheres in Your Home

D1446247

BRENDA KUNNEMAN

received Feb 24, 2022

DESTINY IMAGE® PUBLISHERS, INC.
P.O. Box 310, Shippensburg, PA 17257-0310
"Promoting Inspired Lives."

This book and all other Destiny Image and Destiny Image Fiction books are available at Christian bookstores and distributors worldwide.

Cover design by Eileen Rockwell

For more information on foreign distributors, call 717-532-3040.

Reach us on the Internet: www.destinyimage.com.

ISBN 13 TP: 978-0-7684-5822-0

ISBN 13 eBook: 978-0-7684-5823-7

For Worldwide Distribution, Printed in the U.S.A.

1 2 3 4 5 6 7 8 / 25 24 23 22 21

CONTENTS

INTRODUCTION

I F there is anything that strikes at the heart of most people, it's the wellbeing of their loved ones. With the current condition of our society, many people have become deeply concerned about their family's future and overall wellbeing. But we must remember that God does not want us fearful about our family or our household. God is all about taking care of our families! He is committed to helping your family live a peaceful, abundant, and flourishing life. He is committed to keeping your family intact and causing your home to be a place where He is glorified. God wants your family life and experience to be your greatest joy!

There are many elements that go into making our families and our homelifes strong and successful. It certainly doesn't happen automatically and without dedication. We need to actively invest in our families, and there are many elements involved in that. It requires both spiritual and natural effort; it requires faith and prayer.

Of course, on the natural side, we need to make time for each other, communicate together, and create order and integrity in our homes. Our families should be among our highest priorities. While we know this in principle, it can be difficult because there are many other things in life that demand our time and attention. At the same time, there is also a balance to having a dedicated family investment because it wouldn't be right to spend so much time on family, naturally speaking, that we make little spiritual effort for the Lord or His Kingdom. It's an important balance we must have, and both are needed. Jesus taught the importance of the family investment, but He equally emphasized that His Kingdom must be first, even before family (see Matt. 19:29; Mark 3:33). Why did He emphasize this order? Because without the Lord being first in our focus, all our natural efforts to better our family life become subject to our own imperfections and failures. We must put the spiritual element first in our homes and families so the Lord can intervene in our struggles, help us through tough times, and bring His presence into our homes and families in a tangible way.

One key element people sometimes miss when it comes to putting the spiritual element at the forefront of building strong, stable families is their words and confessions of faith. What we say *to* and *about* our loved ones sets the course for the outcome. If we declare God's Word in faith regarding our family, it brings the Lord's power onto the scene. If we speak words of fear and frustration, it will open the door to the enemy. Our words are powerful tools in building up our family, and we need to prioritize speaking faith-filled words over them. James 3:6 reminds us that our words set nature in motion. This most certainly applies to how we speak to and about our family members. It also applies in how we speak about our homes, our future, and our finances.

In a culture that aims to break down the family structure, we need to speak the right things over our lives and families. We need to verbally take authority over the power of the enemy that would attempt to bring any form of attack or destruction on our families and homes. We have the power to decree and put words into the atmosphere that will bring forth the manifestation of God's supernatural power upon our family life. Our declaration of faith not only sets things in motion both spiritually and naturally, but it also builds our own faith that God is working out His purposes for our loved ones and will not let them fall. Our decree and declaration over our family also serves as a reminder to us that we should not slip into the temptation to speak negatively when it looks in the natural realm like things are turning out opposite of what we desire.

Daily Decrees for Family Blessing and Breakthrough is a tool to help families stand strong in the purposes of God so they can remain unified and experience prosperity and blessing. It will build faith in your spirit that whatever your family faces, God is working a miracle to turn it around for good. Through these declarations, you will also be reminding the enemy that your family, property, and possessions are off-limits and that your family will remain safe and secure! As you decree these words over your loved ones, you are setting nature in motion and establishing a bright future for those you love. It's time to declare blessing and breakthrough over your family!

PEACE IN OUR HOME

DECLARATION

TODAY we decree that our home is filled with God's unsurpassable peace. The atmosphere is saturated with tranquility and serenity. We rely on the Lord's peace, which provides a sense of assurance in our minds and emotions. We declare that we are relaxed and calm. We break the powers of agitation, mayhem, chaos, and disarray in the Name of Jesus! We cast out any evil spirit that would bring disorder to the atmosphere. We declare that those who dwell in our home contribute to peace and do not give place to anything that would create turmoil. We speak that every person who enters our home is enveloped in heavenly peace. We say our home is a place where guests feel the Lord's supernatural rest upon them, and it opens the way for miracles in their lives. We speak great peace upon our home, in the mighty Name of Jesus!

SCRIPTURE

Now the Lord of peace himself give you peace always by all means. The Lord be with you all (2 Thessalonians 3:16).

WORD OF ENCOURAGEMENT

Let's face it, life is busy and there are countless things that can disrupt the peace in our homes. Perhaps you work long hours and, as a result, responsibilities at home tend to fall behind, or maybe you have small children who need constant attention. In addition, there can be things like health issues and financial challenges that can rob our homes of peace. But the good news is the Lord is the giver of peace! He can extend a supernatural peace that can squelch the mayhem that would seek to invade your house. I want to encourage you to declare peace over your home. Along with that, work to create a peaceful home environment. Things like eliminating clutter, reducing excess noise, and increasing general organization can all contribute to improving peace. Remember, we do what we can both in the natural realm and the spiritual realm to walk in the peace the Lord wants us to experience. The key is not to allow life to rob the Lord's peace from your house!

WE WILL SERVE THE LORD

DECLARATION

TODAY we declare that all who live in our home serve the Lord. We prophesy that each member of this household honors God in word, action, and deed. We are a family who gives the Lord the place of supreme rule, and we choose to uphold His Word and commandments. His Name shall always be reverenced under our roof. We speak words of praise and esteem about the Lord. We speak that in this home the Lord is high and lifted up, and His presence fills every room! We say that no antichrist spirit is able to operate in this house. We break the power of any opposing spirit or influence, and we close the door to all things that dishonor our God. We decree that the banner written upon the doorposts of this house is, "As for me and my house, we serve the Lord!"

SCRIPTURE

And if it seem evil unto you to serve the Lord, choose you this day whom ye will serve; whether the gods which your fathers served that were on the other side of the flood, or the gods of the Amorites, in whose land ye dwell: but as for me and my house, we will serve the Lord (Joshua 24:15).

WORD OF ENCOURAGEMENT

One of the most important things a family can do is decide that their home will be a place where God is honored. This means that anything that would dishonor the Lord is not allowed access to the premises; all that is said and done carries the Lord's honor upon it. Moses taught the children of Israel that they were to teach their children to praise and honor God in everything they did. This was not to be a one-time decision. It was something they acknowledged in an ongoing way. There is so much in our culture that dishonors God today and, over time, it can be easy to unintentionally allow things to creep into our homes that are in opposition to the Lord. Regularly making the verbal declaration—that your house will be one that gives God the preeminence in everything—will ensure your home remains free of the things that would bring dishonor to Him!

TIME FOR
TOGETHERNESS

DECLARATION

TODAY we declare that our home is filled with oneness, togetherness, unity, and fellowship. Our home is characterized by a closeness and affection between all who live and visit here. We love to be together, talk, interact, and communicate with one another. We are a family that enjoys fun activities without distraction or interruption. We say that nothing can disrupt our family time and the closeness we share in this home. We break the power of all evil spirits that would come to separate, divide, distract, or invade our togetherness, in Jesus' Name! We prophesy that we have our schedules, plans, and activities in order so that an atmosphere of unity thrives and we can spend time together without disruption or distraction. We say that we are a household of togetherness and we are a family of closeness!

SCRIPTURE

Behold, how good and how pleasant it is for brethren to dwell together in unity! (Psalm 133:1)

WORD OF ENCOURAGEMENT

If you are like many families, you already know the challenges that can arise to keep you from spending quality time with your loved ones. You also know there are countless things that can creep in to create separation until everyone is so busy doing their own thing that they're doing nothing together. Family togetherness is the quest of nearly every family that exists, and it's something to be fought for and protected. Make it a goal to develop quality family time, while simultaneously considering what you can eliminate that might disrupt family togetherness. Too often a sense of closeness isn't just built by what we do; it's also built by what we remove. For example, too many hours at work will eventually take its toll on family time. It's also important to consider that a sense of togetherness can be easily increased through simple, meaningful, and regular conversation.

Phone calls, kind notes, and thoughtful gestures all lead to feelings of closeness. Lastly, avoid speaking words of division or expressing continual feelings of frustration. Instead, declare togetherness and allow it to permeate the atmosphere of your home!

AN ORDERLY ENVIRONMENT

DECLARATION

TODAY we prophesy that we live lives of order. We say that we live in a home that is decent and orderly. We say that our household is run and operated in a tidy, organized, and constructed manner. We live in a clean and safe environment. We declare that no evil spirits of disorder, disarray, filth, or mayhem can operate here, in Jesus' Name! Our home is free of all hazards, pitfalls, risks, and peril. We do not allow our home to be in ill repair. We prophesy that we have the wisdom and insight to create functionality in every room of our home. We enjoy an inviting, pleasant atmosphere throughout our house and say it's a place where we love to spend our time. We speak that heaven's decorum is represented in our home and all who enter here see the excellence that characterizes our place of habitation.

SCRIPTURE

Let all things be done decently and in order
(1 Corinthians 14:40).

WORD OF ENCOURAGEMENT

While the context of the Scripture above is about the local church assembly, it's also a general truth which reveals that God expects the environments we inhabit to be characterized by order. Whether it be our place of business, our home, or our churches, God wants there to be visible order in all we do because we are His representatives. We should reflect the order of heaven because heaven is an orderly place. This isn't to say we need to be perfect and that each room in our house shouldn't have a single thing out of place. Let's face it, we live real lives and messes happen! However, we shouldn't be constantly surrounded by a cluttered mess. This way of living discredits us and isn't a good testimony to the Lord. When the Queen of Sheba came to visit Solomon, the Bible notes that she was not only impacted by the opulence of Solomon's house, but she was particularly impacted by the excellence and order of how his kingdom functioned (see 1 Kings 10:1-5). Of course, we don't have to live opulent lives like King Solomon to create order; we can create an inviting environment in the humblest place of living. What's important is that God is a God of order, and we can't disregard the fact that this is part of His nature. We should strive for an environment of order in all we do. Speaking and decreeing order in your life is a great way to develop the consciousness to create it. And at the end of the day, there isn't a person on earth who doesn't enjoy clean and orderly surroundings!

GLORY IN THE
ATMOSPHERE

DECLARATION

WE decree that an atmosphere of God's glory floods our home. We speak and say that the presence of the Lord is everywhere. We call for the cloud of God's *Shekinah* glory to invade every room and crevice of our house. May every person who enters here be affected by the glory of the Lord. Because of the atmosphere of glory, we receive the goodness of the Lord, even as Moses saw God's goodness when he encountered the glory. We take authority over any demonic interference that would squelch the atmosphere of glory. We prophesy that in the glory we are changed, healed, and delivered. We submit ourselves to whatever the Holy Spirit wants to accomplish. We avail ourselves of spending time in the Lord's presence, and we allow the glory to rest upon our lives. Lord, we thank You that Your glory permeates us and is welcome in our house. Like Moses, we ask to see Your glory and we want to experience it daily in our home!

SCRIPTURE

I beseech thee, shew me thy glory (Exodus 33:18).

WORD OF ENCOURAGEMENT

The encounter between God and Moses in Exodus 33 is undoubtedly one of the most impactful biblical encounters between God and a human being. It was an expression of a man who wanted to be entirely immersed in the awesome presence of Almighty God. Moses' yearning was so intense that he literally begged for the Lord to allow His glory to be visible. In other words, Moses wanted to see God with his eyes!

Today we are not much different than Moses in our desire to see the Lord. Yes, we want to see Him with our eyes, but we also want to experience Him in every aspect of our being. We express this desire by saying, "I want to experience the glory!" In that, we want our homes to be a place where the glory of the Lord is present and felt by those who live in and enter our home. We want our homes to be a place where people come and literally sense the Lord.

If you want to have the Lord's glory in the atmosphere of your house, then it needs to be cherished and protected. Be careful not to allow things that squelch the glory or interfere with it. Consider the things you read or watch on TV or electronic devices. Ensure that your actions do not hinder the presence of His glory. Then make the point to invite the Lord's glory to have its welcomed place around you on a regular basis. Ask the Lord for the atmosphere of glory to be in your home!

GOD'S GOODNESS
REIGNS HERE!

DECLARATION

WE decree that we live under the umbrella of God's immeasurable goodness. His goodness reigns in our home. We live each day experiencing His goodness, grace, and mercy. We prophesy that His goodness shall pass before us as it did Moses, and we shall be placed upon the rock of a sure foundation. In our house, we declare that the Lord is good and His mercy endures forever. We do not focus on the negatives, disappointments, and setbacks. We break the power of any evil spirit that would come to cloud our minds and prevent us from seeing the good. We make the decision as a household to promote the good, see the good, and speak about the good acts of God in our lives. We prophesy that surely goodness and mercy shall follow us all the days of our life and that evil cannot track us! We speak that we shall experience good things from the Lord in the days ahead and it will cause us to rejoice and shout for joy! May the goodness of the Lord always reign in our hearts, reign in our lives, and reign in our home, in Jesus' Name!

SCRIPTURE

And he said, I will make all my goodness pass before thee, and I will proclaim the name of the Lord before thee; and will be gracious to whom I will be gracious, and will shew mercy on whom I will shew mercy (Exodus 33:19).

WORD OF ENCOURAGEMENT

One of the greatest things God wants His people to understand about His character is that He is good! Too often, religion teaches us to see God's judgment and wrath. While God does exhibit judgment simply because He is just, we must also know that God isn't recklessly raining judgment upon people. In fact, you often hear people question why so much evil in the world seems to go on unchecked and God seemingly doesn't do anything. Why doesn't God just step in to stop it? Because He is a good God! He is giving people everywhere the opportunity to repent and turn to Him. This isn't to say evildoers will not eventually be judged; we all *do* reap what we sow (see Gal. 6:7). However, God wants to give people as much time as possible to turn away from evil. We see further revelation about this at the birth of Jesus, when the angels made the proclamation, "Peace on earth, goodwill toward men" (see Luke 2:14). The angels were announcing that because of Jesus, God's hand of wrath was being stayed until the appointed time.

The important thing is to see that God is good! He *wants* to extend goodness to humanity, and He wants to extend His goodness toward you! Begin each day expecting His goodness to surround you and know that this is what He is proclaiming upon you and your family!

UNITY AND
AGREEMENT AMONG US

DECLARATION

TODAY we decree that unity and agreement reigns in our home. We prophesy that we work together in harmony in all we do. We say that the anointing of the Lord comes to bring us into one accord and that we work as a unified family under the governance of the Word of God. We agree with God's Word and therefore agree together on our plans, decisions, ideals, calling, and purpose. We agree on how to govern our family and manage our occupations. We agree on where to live, what to buy, when to move, and where to fellowship. We agree regarding all things that are relevant to life and godliness. We are unified in our stance that evil has no place in our lives. We are one, under the command of our Lord Jesus Christ. We break the power of all disunity, discord, and conflict, in the Name of Jesus! We speak unity, oneness, harmony, and peace. We humble ourselves under the Lord's

DAILY DECREES FOR FAMILY BLESSING AND BREAKTHROUGH

almighty hand and we submit ourselves to one another in the bond of peace. May a supernatural spirit of agreement reside upon us that causes us to build our lives as a strong family unit. We declare unity and agreement is among us!

SCRIPTURE

Behold, how good and how pleasant it is for brethren to dwell together in unity! (Psalm 133:1)

WORD OF ENCOURAGEMENT

One of the most challenging things that a family or household can face is when its members are not unified in the key issues of life. When a married couple, or even families with older children still at home, find themselves going in multiple directions, it can wreak havoc. A good example is when one person feels a strong conviction about something that another doesn't share. One person believes the family should go down a certain path and the other one isn't convinced. In some cases, one person is serving God while their spouse or children are unbelieving. One of the primary ways to build household agreement is by focusing on the areas where agreement already exists and build upon them. Learn to emphasize the things you do agree on. Too often as people, we allow ourselves to focus on the areas where we differ, and this only serves to magnify disunity. Sure, families or married couples may not agree on every point, but the key is to make a practice of agreement. Search for agreement and look for ways to defer to the other person or people in your home in a way that values their thoughts and ideas. Learn to listen and hear the heart of each person and then begin to speak and declare unity. Believe God that your plans and ideas will be yoked together in a heavenly way and that He will cause your entire household to be on an overall path of agreement and unity.

EFFECTIVE
COMMUNICATION ESTABLISHED

DECLARATION

W E decree that effective communication is established in our home. We prophesy that we are skilled communicators and we grow in our ability to converse and articulate our thoughts. We declare according to the Word of God that we are quick to hear, slow to speak, and slow to anger. We say that we are able to control our tongues and we only speak what is good and edifying to those who hear. We declare that we have the skill to hear the hearts and minds of others through what they say, and we don't jump to conclusions or misconstrue their words. We break the power of all manner of confusion, misunderstanding, and misjudgment. We declare that each member of our household feels accepted, understood, and appreciated for their thoughts and values. We say our minds are open to receive and absorb what others are communicating whether in thought, word, or deed.

We say that our home is a place where quality communication flows freely and fluently, in Jesus' mighty Name!

SCRIPTURE

Let your speech be always with grace, seasoned with salt, that ye may know how ye ought to answer every man (Colossians 4:6).

WORD OF ENCOURAGEMENT

Every successful relationship needs effective communication. In fact, one of the reasons many people turn to professional counseling is communication problems. We must understand that communication isn't always verbal; it's also our actions, attitude, and behavior. In fact, commonly in the King James Version of the Bible we see the word *conversation* used (see Eph. 4:22; Phil. 1:27), which today we associate with verbal communication. However, the word actually means *behavior.* What we do and how we act are forms of conversation. A person who is a skilled communicator typically isn't the person doing all the speaking. Skilled communicators spend more time listening and absorbing information so that when they do speak, they are filled with substance and viable information rather than assumptions. If we want our family relationships to be healthy, we must become good communicators. This comes more naturally for some than others, but we must make the point to develop in this capacity. Begin by declaring that effective communication prevails in your family. Then make the point to practice what good communicators do—listen, appreciate, and then pause before responding. Behave in a mannerly way that communicates positively to those you love. Every house can have effective communication established among every member of the family!

RICHES IN
OUR HOUSE

DECLARATION

WE decree that the riches and the provision of the Lord fills our house. We say that we will never lack any form of wealth to meet our physical and material needs. We are confident in the covenant promise that wealth and riches shall be in the house of the righteous and there is no lack to those who love the Lord. We prophesy increase and overflow. We declare that we always have more than enough so that we can be a blessing to others and to the Kingdom of God. We give of our wealth and, therefore, we are confident that the Lord will give back to us through the hands of people according to Luke 6:38. We decree that everything that is in our heart to accomplish financially under the Lord's direction, we are able to accomplish. We break the power of lack and decrease and prophesy that no spirit of decay or corruption can come to rob our wealth because we have treasure stored in heaven! We stand in the confidence that our house experiences abundance today, and every day throughout the years to come, in Jesus' Name! Wealth and riches are in our house!

SCRIPTURE

Wealth and riches shall be in his house: and his righteousness endureth for ever (Psalm 112:3).

WORD OF ENCOURAGEMENT

I once heard a man say, "There are few pressures in life that compare to financial pressure." To a great extent, that is true. Money can have a tremendous effect on how people think and behave. It is often the source of fear and anxiety, particularly when a household or business is struggling to make ends meet. It's hard not to get one's eyes on the circumstances when the bills keep piling up. But this is *not* the will of God for His people! Financial stress and lack are not of God—they come from the enemy! We have a covenant promise that wealth and riches shall be in the house of the righteous. Know without any shadow of doubt that this is God's will for you and your family. There are countless scriptures that remind us of not only God's provision, but His willingness to make that provision abundant. Walking in this promise comes by believing it with unshakable faith. First, make sure you are following the biblical parameters and requirements for handling your money. Tithe and give offerings as the Word of God teaches. Tithing, in and of itself, is an expression of your confidence in the Lord's provision. Second, practice good money-handling skills and know what the Bible says about mishandling of money. Then finally, speak and declare the promises of provision instead of speaking lack! All of the above can set you in a place to receive God's promise of wealth and riches miraculously resting over your house!

AN ATMOSPHERE
FOR MIRACLES

DECLARATION

WE decree that our home is an atmosphere where miracles operate and manifest regularly. We declare that we receive divine experiences and supernatural encounters from heaven. We receive manifestations that turn impossible situations around and bring blessing and surprises. People get healed in our home and receive instantaneous miracles. We declare the manifestation of miracles, signs, and wonders flows freely. We say that signs follow the Word of God that is spoken and preached in our home. We invite the supernatural presence of the Lord to take up residence here. We break the power of all hindrances, unbelief, and religious spirits that would discount miracles, and we prophesy that our minds are open and receptive to the supernatural move of God. We are a family who creates the atmosphere of miracles in our home, in Jesus' Name!

SCRIPTURE

And the disciples went everywhere and preached, and the Lord worked through them, confirming what they said by many miraculous signs (Mark 16:20 NLT).

WORD OF ENCOURAGEMENT

Many believers do not fully understand the miraculous side of God, particularly when it comes to receiving miracles in their own lives. People often do not progress beyond the realm of guessing what God will do about their situation, or if and when they will experience the miracle they're desiring. The age-old question of why some people receive a miracle and others do not remains difficult to answer because not all situations are exactly the same. However, we *do* know this: We *can* create an environment that sets the atmosphere for miracles. We see this in the ministry of Jesus. People who received miracles from Him were in a place of faith for such; they were anticipating that they would receive (see Matt. 8:13; Mark 5:34; 9:23). On the flip side, when Jesus came to Nazareth, He was unable to do any mighty works because of their unbelief (see Mark 6:5). They resisted and analyzed Jesus' miracle-working power and, as a result, they did not receive. We must be people who create an atmosphere that is receptive to God's miracle-working power. We do so by believing for it, not by analyzing it logically and ultimately rejecting it, like the people of Nazareth. Instead, talk about miracles in your home. When you pray, tell the Lord how much you believe in His miracle power. Build your faith on the Word of God that reveals how willing He is to exercise His miraculous nature on your behalf. Declare that your home is filled with miracles, and always speak accordingly. Lastly, avoid unbelief and speaking negatively when circumstances seem adverse and it doesn't appear that God will step in. Your home *is* a place for miracles!

GATHERINGS OF JOY!

DECLARATION

W E declare that times of celebration, holidays, family gatherings, and vacations are times of joy for our family! We prophesy that special occasions are peaceful, positive, refreshing, and cheerful. We speak that these memorable times are something we will always cherish in our hearts and will be remembered dearly. We declare that all planning for such events and gatherings shall be stress-free and strife-free. We break the power of any spirits of darkness that would interrupt our family memories or create division, in Jesus' Name. We speak that we are able to celebrate without fear, care, or worry. We prophesy that birthdays, barbeques, graduations, dinners, luncheons, holidays, and vacations are all blessed, safe, prosperous, and festive. We call upon the Lord God to place the shadow of His wing upon us so that all is well whenever we gather with family or friends. We say that our family *always* experiences gatherings of joy, in the Name of Jesus!

SCRIPTURE

For the despondent, every day brings trouble; for the happy heart, life is a continual feast (Proverbs 15:15 NLT).

WORD OF ENCOURAGEMENT

Special family events and gatherings are something we look forward to throughout the year, or at least we should! Sometimes the burden of planning or dealing with family issues can turn what is meant to be a joyous occasion into a stressful one. Preventing that from happening begins with approaching these special occasions with the confidence that they will turn out right! Our attitude must be set correctly in advance. The scripture above reminds us that when our mindset is negative, we invite trouble. But when our hearts are happy, we live in a place of joyous feasting, even when extended family occasionally adds drama and difficulty! We must trust that God can enable us to live above those things so we can enjoy all the good things that family brings to our lives. Rather than allowing the enemy to interrupt your special times, begin to declare in advance what these times shall be so the Lord and His presence can prevail in the atmosphere. Stand in faith that stress will be quelled and your gatherings will *always* be filled with joy!

A NO-FLY ZONE!

DECLARATION

WE decree that our house is a no-fly zone to the operations of the enemy! Just as the children of Israel were separated by God from the plague of flies that came upon the Egyptians, so are we protected from every plague of the enemy. No evil forces, plots, plans, or works of demonic spirits can access the premises of our house. We say that the doors to our home are never entered by any entity that is in opposition to God. We break the power of any spells, incantations, or hexes from any witch, warlock, or worker of divination, in Jesus' Name. We prophesy that no plague, pestilence, accident, tragedy, calamity, mischief, or mayhem is allowed to enter here, in the Name of Jesus! All forces of darkness and evil must cease and desist from any maneuver or operation being attempted against this household. Our house is protected by the blood of Jesus that is upon its doorposts. A divine hedge surrounds our property and the angels of the

Most High are standing guard. We live in safety and peace because our house is a no-fly zone to the enemy!

SCRIPTURE

And I will sever in that day the land of Goshen, in which my people dwell, that no swarms of flies shall be there; to the end thou mayest know that I am the Lord in the midst of the earth (Exodus 8:22).

WORD OF ENCOURAGEMENT

When God sent the ten plagues upon Egypt, the Bible doesn't specify that the Lord separated the Israelites who lived in Goshen from the Egyptians until the fourth plague, the swarm of flies. While this isn't to say the plagues were *in* Goshen, it's not clear whether the Israelites working amongst the Egyptians weren't equally affected by the first three plagues. But we know that when the flies came, God brought a divine separation between the Egyptians and the children of Israel. This is important—it helps us to see that we can trust God to separate His people from the world.

Part of that separation includes a separation of favor, protection, and increase. Have confidence today that the Lord is separating you and your family from all the mayhem in the world. Declare today and every day that your home is a "no-fly zone" to all the enemy's operations!

PERSONAL
GROWTH AND DEVELOPMENT

DECLARATION

W E declare that as a family, we grow in the grace and knowledge of God. We decree that we are always advancing in our spiritual understanding and divine insight. We prophesy that we are a household immersed in the Word of God and we do what the Bible commands. We give of ourselves to do all that is needed to become mature saints. We declare spiritual growth, improvement, and expansion. We declare that we grow in prayer and study. We prophesy that we are mature and stable believers who function effectively within the Body of Christ. We say that nothing shall come to hinder, abort, or stunt the process of maturity in any member of our family! We decree that each of us grows spiritually in all aspects that the Lord desires for us, in Jesus' Name!

SCRIPTURE

But grow in grace, and in the knowledge of our Lord and Saviour Jesus Christ. To him be glory both now and for ever. Amen (2 Peter 3:18).

WORD OF ENCOURAGEMENT

There probably isn't a more important element to our Christianity than our personal growth in the Lord. God wants us to develop beyond spiritual babyhood into mature saints. This needs to be a quest that we take seriously each day. By speaking and declaring over our own spiritual growth process, we become cognizant that this task is always before us. A mature believer who is constantly progressing in their spiritual development is a believer who can handle difficulty, face tribulation, and remain stable in the journey. Immaturity causes us to become reactionary to whatever the circumstance is at a given moment. This immaturity is often expressed through careless words, whereas a mature person knows how to control their tongue and choose their words wisely. A mature believer will ensure that they are committed to walking in all the commandments of Scripture. They are also dedicated to maintaining a teachable spirit that is receptive to the instruction and input of others. Take the position that you will commit to spiritual maturity, not only by doing the things necessary to obtaining it, but by declaring it upon your life and upon your family!

GOD'S WILL
ESTABLISHED

DECLARATION

TODAY we decree that the will of God is known and established in our lives. We declare that we walk in the good, acceptable, and perfect will of God in all things. As a family, we will not miss the mark, get off track, or fall outside of God's will for us. We prophesy that any distractions, interferences, or diversions that would seduce us away from God's perfect plan are rendered powerless, in the Name of Jesus! We declare that our hearts and minds hear the will of God with clarity and accuracy. We do not hear the voice of a stranger because we are the Lord's sheep who hear His voice! We prophesy, let the Lord's Kingdom come, let His will be done in our lives as it is in heaven. We call the will of God for us into full manifestation, and we declare that the will and purpose of God for us manifests each and every day!

SCRIPTURE

And he said unto them, When ye pray, say, Our Father which art in heaven, Hallowed be thy name. Thy kingdom come. Thy will be done, as in heaven, so in earth (Luke 11:2).

WORD OF ENCOURAGEMENT

There is not a Christian on earth who does not want to live their life in God's perfect will. Just the thought of being out of God's will can cause great anxiety for a true believer. We want to know God's will regarding our occupations, where we live, the friends we connect with, and the person we should marry. The good news is, God isn't making His will a mystery! He wants us to know His will clearly. Walking in His perfect will first begins with knowing what the Bible commands and making every effort to obey Scripture. Begin with what Scripture is clear on, and then allow the Holy Spirit to lead you in the things the Bible isn't specific about, such as what occupation to choose or some other specific decision. Many times, when we find ourselves out of God's will, we can look back and learn that God was showing us not to take that route all along. However, we can be assured that for those who truly care about being in God's will, the Lord will always circle us right back in line with where we need to be. Regularly declaring that you walk in His perfect will will cause you to stay alert so that you don't get away from His divine plan!

GRACE THAT PREVAILS

DECLARATION

TODAY we declare and prophesy that we receive a multiplication of grace. We have access by faith into heavenly grace that grants us divine favor. We receive the grace that forgives, restores, heals, and blesses. We say that every challenge we face is overcome by divine grace that enables us to rise above every problem. We reject any spirit of condemnation, opposition, or disapproval, and we say that it cannot interfere with the grace upon us, in the Name of Jesus. We declare double grace and favor and receive God's grace that is more than enough. We say not by might, nor by power, but by the Spirit of the Lord we live in total breakthrough! We speak to every mountain in our way and say that it will become a plain as we shout GRACE, GRACE to it! We are a family who trusts in and relies upon the grace of God that sees us through to victory in every situation!

SCRIPTURE

Then he answered and spake unto me, saying, This is the word of the Lord unto Zerubbabel, saying, Not by might, nor by power, but by my spirit, saith the Lord of hosts. Who art thou, O great mountain? before Zerubbabel thou shalt become a plain: and he shall bring forth the headstone thereof with shoutings, crying, Grace, grace unto it (Zechariah 4:6-7).

WORD OF ENCOURAGEMENT

In the Christian world, the word *grace* is often used loosely. People sometimes use it without fully grasping its powerful meaning. Yes, we understand the word in its simplest form means *unmerited favor*. However, what we sometimes forget is the supernatural element behind the word. Grace is a word that reveals God's willingness to fight on our behalf to bring us into victory, no matter what difficulty we face in life. That is why Zechariah could shout grace to the mountain and expect it to come down before his eyes. In a sense, this is perhaps why we do use the word loosely or freely. It's because grace covers *everything*. It touches every need with a breakthrough, a miracle, and a blessing. The grace of God upon your life will cause you to prevail every time, in every situation. This is a great day to shout, "Grace! Grace!"

UNDERSTANDING
AND COMPASSION

DECLARATION

WE decree that we are family of understanding and compassion. We are considerate of one another and show each other the love of Christ Jesus in every circumstance. We exhibit care, responsibility, and tenderness toward the needs of others. We tend to each other and serve one another. We take upon ourselves the burdens of others and are quick to jump in and alleviate the needs that our other family members may have. We prophesy that we are a family that is courteous, caring, and that looks upon the concerns of others before we consider ourselves. We demonstrate affectionate love. We declare that all hardness of heart, callousness, or neglect of any kind is not once named among us. We declare that each day we exhibit the understanding and compassion of our Lord Jesus Christ.

SCRIPTURE

Finally, be ye all of one mind, having compassion one of another, love as brethren, be pitiful, be courteous (1 Peter 3:8).

WORD OF ENCOURAGEMENT

It's not hard to see that today's culture is one where people are becoming increasingly careless and hardhearted. Second Timothy 3:3 says that in the last days, people will be "without natural affection." This simply means people will lose the natural art of human kindness. Instead, they will become calloused to the plight of others. Jesus made a similar statement when He said the love of many will wax cold (see Matt. 24:12). We see this type of behavior displayed quite clearly in the ways people comment on social media platforms. So much commentary is filled with vile hatred and shaming of others. As believers, we must resist the tide of the culture that is overwhelming so many people in this way. We must do the opposite and become examples of God's compassion. This must begin in our homes, with how we treat our family members. We need to practice the care and consideration of our family and work to make our home a place where we exhibit understanding and compassion. Doing it at home will cause it to spill over into the rest of society and will be a testimony of Jesus to a hurting world. This is God's will for us. Declare that you and those in your home are people of understanding and compassion!

STRIFE
IS BROKEN!

DECLARATION

TODAY we break the power of strife over our home and our family! We decree our home is an environment where strife has no place and no voice. We rebuke all demonic powers that would create contention, bickering, quarrels, and altercations, in the Name of Jesus. We say that we refuse to be lured into strife-filled conversations and situations. We declare that anger, contention, touchiness, grouchiness, temper tantrums, and flare-ups are not allowed in our home. We prophesy that we are a family who controls our emotions, words, and attitudes and we submit them to the Lordship of Jesus Christ. We say strife is replaced with patience and self-control. We do not stir up strife with our actions, and we choose to create a home that is strife-free and contention-free. We prophesy that in our family and home the power of strife is broken!

SCRIPTURE

A hot-tempered person stirs up strife, but the slow to anger calms a dispute (Proverbs 15:18 NASB).

WORD OF ENCOURAGEMENT

No one enjoys contention or contentious conversations. Resolving differences considerately is very different from allowing strife to run freely through your household. Most strife arises when those involved have a difficult time controlling feelings, attitudes, and the like. It usually results in sharp tones of voice, sarcastic comments, or rude body language. Strife must be a bigger problem than we'd like to think, because so many Scripture verses, particularly in the New Testament, address avoiding strife and contention. When we realize that being a strife-filled, contentious person doesn't please God, we know that we need to avoid strife at all costs. Strife not only hurts those around us, but it robs our day of joy and fulfillment. Demonic spirits love to stir up strife, so we must not become ensnared by them! A key to learning how to be a person devoid of strife is to speak over yourself that the power of strife will not be allowed to rule over you or take control of the environment in your house. Declaring strife is broken will remind you not to stir up strife when the opportunity arises, but rather to do the opposite and maintain peace!

FINANCIAL
PROVISION AND INCREASE

DECLARATION

W E decree that we live in a constant place of financial provision and increase. We live under that continual fountain of heavenly supply. We say that each year our finances grow to another level of increase and abundance. We break the power of decrease and decline, in the Name of Jesus! We break the power of bankruptcy, deficiency, and depletion. We prophesy that financial distress and crisis of every kind is replaced with financial contentment and stability. We say that we receive regular boosts and raises and that no bill goes unpaid. We will always have more than enough, excess, and overflow, and every need we will ever have shall be provided for, in Jesus' Name!

SCRIPTURE

The blessing of the Lord, it maketh rich, and he addeth no sorrow with it (Proverbs 10:22).

WORD OF ENCOURAGEMENT

Many believers have a hard time envisioning God providing them financial sufficiency that goes above and beyond just getting by. In fact, too often people are content to live well below what the Lord really wants for them. But consider the many ways that financial deficiency is not a blessing! It creates stress and hardship, yet many believers simply accept it. In saying this, some will automatically retort, "Yes, but the apostle Paul encouraged that we should know how to live both in sufficiency and also in need!" (see Phil. 4:12). While it's true that we need to maintain the same position of faith in times when lack tries to arise, Paul wasn't implying that we are to be accepting of lack. He was teaching that in all times, we must keep our faith engaged for a breakthrough and not give up when we face difficulties. God wants us to experience constant financial provision, and that is what we should set our faith upon. Jesus said He came to give life and life *more* abundantly (see John 10:10). Of course, this verse doesn't only refer to financial provision, but it's definitely part of the package! Include financial provision in your daily declarations. Begin to see yourself on a constant track of increase and refuse to accept decrease and lack. If the Lord wants you to be supplied, then the key is to get in agreement with God and expect financial provision!

LIFTED
HEARTS

DECLARATION

WE decree today that our hearts are lifted up and our countenance is raised and encouraged. We declare relief, assistance, and comfort upon our household. We prophesy that our morale is boosted in the face of every challenge. We break the power of anything that would cause us to be cast down, discouraged, depressed, sad, or unhappy, in Jesus' Name. We declare that we believe the report of the Lord and will not believe any negative report. We resist and reject the emotional effect of bad news and disappointment. We look past every problem and we see the answer and the light at the end of the tunnel. We choose to see the joy that is before us. We envision all things being bright and going well for our family. We place our eyes on the Lord who is the lifter of our hearts!

SCRIPTURE

When men are cast down, then thou shalt say, There is lifting up; and he shall save the humble person (Job 22:29).

WORD OF ENCOURAGEMENT

One of the greatest, most powerful skills a believer can possess is the ability to maintain a position of faith and stamina when something negative is trying to close in. Keeping your emotions in check and not allowing yourself to get down and discouraged is something you must actively fight for. Our emotions can be affected by the slightest things. Something like a simple change in the weather can affect attitudes and emotions, so we need to be careful not to let our hearts get heavy. It's important in such times to remind ourselves that the Lord is also in the business of lifting up our hearts in times when we feel down. We need to see it as a supernatural thing. It's not something we have to just muster up on our own. We can ask the Lord to lift us up, give us a boost in our thinking, and help us to see things aren't as bad as they might appear. The Lord will also enable us look past any current problems and see a victory, just as Jesus was able to do when He went to the Cross—He saw the joy on the other side (see Heb. 12:2). Stand strong today and know that the Lord is lifting your heart!

SUCCESSFUL
ENDEAVORS

DECLARATION

TODAY we decree that our endeavors and undertakings are filled with progress and success. As a family, we are well able to finish everything we start, and every plan from heaven given to us to accomplish shall be completed with quality. We resist and reject any spirit that would bring defeat, failure, forfeiture, or loss, in Jesus' Name. We declare nothing shall come to halt or terminate the projects before us. We say that all our dreams and goals given by God come to fruition. Whatever we set our hand to do shall prosper and the Lord shall bless all the work of our hands. We prophesy that we possess the ability to bring forth innovative ideas into reality. We speak success over our household and say that every member of our family is able to accomplish all that God has given them to do, in the Name of Jesus.

SCRIPTURE

The Lord shall command the blessing upon thee in thy storehouses, and in all that thou settest thine hand unto; and he shall bless thee in the land which the Lord thy God giveth thee (Deuteronomy 28:8).

WORD OF ENCOURAGEMENT

Every one of us has probably had the experience of starting a project or goal only to have it interrupted and not get completed. Regardless of the reason, it's disappointing, particularly when a great deal of time and/or money was invested. But being unable to complete goals and projects shouldn't be our story as believers. Sometimes interference occurs because we need to grow in how we handle our time, money, or ideas. In other cases, the enemy comes to bring interruptions to our efforts and to disrupt our plans. Nevertheless, one of God's most powerful promises is that if we serve Him wholeheartedly, He will bring success to our endeavors, no matter what the enemy may try. God wants us to be successful, not so we can boast in ourselves, but so we can bring honor and glory to Him. Today the Holy Spirit wants to liberate you and your family from any feelings of failure that may have arisen when something you set out to accomplish didn't come to fruition. God wants you to feel a new sense of accomplishment today that through His power and strength, all the members of your household can experience successful endeavors.

DEBT CANCELLATION

DECLARATION

WE decree that we experience debt cancellations and bills being supernaturally paid. We declare that we are debt-free! We break the power of debt and indebtedness. We say that we shall not enter into unnecessary debt, but we also prophesy that no debt that is beyond our control can come upon our household. We declare every demonic spirit that would drive us into debt is bound, in Jesus' Name. We say that we are prosperous and able to live a debt-free lifestyle. We are able to lend and help others in need. We are blessed to be a blessing and help alleviate the debts of others. We say this day that debts are decreasing and cancelled until we are completely out of debt, in the Name of Jesus!

SCRIPTURE

And thou shalt lend unto many nations, and thou shalt not borrow (Deuteronomy 28:12).

WORD OF ENCOURAGEMENT

The majority of debt most people carry is created due to poor spending habits. However, there is debt that people sometimes incur that is truly out of their control. For example, a large, unexpected repair or medical bill may create a debt situation. Debt can be stressful and put a tremendous weight on people's finances. Descending into debt is something we know we should avoid, but we also know God can, and often does, supernaturally intervene to cancel debt. We need to have faith for that! Many believers have experienced bills being paid off in supernatural ways that only the Lord could have accomplished! Whether the debt you are facing was self-created or out of your control, ask your heavenly Father to help you get out of debt, both through your natural efforts and by His supernatural help and power. Remember, we serve a loving and gracious God who wants to help us. Live your life in faith that you can be free from debt. By declaring a debt-free lifestyle over you and your family, you will create the consciousness to avoid debt and build your faith for the Lord to deliver you from debt, both now and in the future! Declare debt cancellation, in Jesus' Name!

RESTFUL SLEEP

DECLARATION

WE decree that every member of our household and family experiences nights of restful sleep. We prophesy an atmosphere of complete peace and tranquility in our home that enables us to sleep soundly every night. We break the power of all sleep disorders, insomnia, sleep apnea, restlessness, discomfort, nightmares, anxieties, fears, and imbalances, in the Name of Jesus. We declare no evil spirit can interject itself while our family is asleep. We reject and resist anything that would disrupt our sleep, and we prophesy that our regular sleep schedule is well-established and stays on track. We decree that we have the wisdom to create an environment that promotes rest and comfort. We prophesy that we have divine dreams, heavenly visitations, and visions while we sleep. We ask the Lord to give us restful sleep so that every day we awake refreshed, rejuvenated, and filled with renewed energy! We say that every member of our family is able to sleep peacefully and that we experience continual nights of uninterrupted, restful sleep!

SCRIPTURE

It is vain for you to rise up early, to sit up late, to eat the bread of sorrows: for so he giveth his beloved sleep (Psalm 127:2).

WORD OF ENCOURAGEMENT

With entire medical studies, industries, and countless products dedicated to the sleep experience, it's undisputed that a good night's rest is paramount to our quality of life. A lack of proper sleep leads to medical problems, depression, and an overall lack of productivity, just to name a few. It's important to do what you can in the natural to help promote sleep. Keeping a schedule and regular bedtime where possible, creating the right atmosphere, and proper bedding are all things that help promote rest. However, sometimes sleep is interrupted by the forces of the enemy. Satan loves to attack people when they are sleeping by invading them with fears, nightmares, or medically related problems that disrupt their sleep. What we must know is that God *gives* His beloved sleep. Just as the enemy can try to interrupt sleep, the Lord can bring a supernatural sleep upon you. Before retiring at night, declare that you will have a night of restful and uninterrupted sleep and nothing shall interfere with it, in Jesus' Name.

OVERWHELMING PRESENCE

DECLARATION

W E decree that the overwhelming presence of the Lord rests in our home. His presence causes us to experience joy and to rejoice every day. The Lord's presence in our lives and home transcends every circumstance and situation. We cannot hide from the Lord's presence and He is with us wherever we go. His presence upon us breaks the power of all manner of bondage and strongholds. We prophesy that no form of demonic oppression can reside in our home because the presence of the Lord drives it out. Just as the mountains melt like wax at the presence of the Lord, so do any obstacles in our lives. We declare that we experience complete freedom and liberty because of the presence of the Lord. We come into His presence with rejoicing and singing. We constantly search for ways to experience His presence in our lives. We decree that the overwhelming presence of the Lord is upon our family now!

SCRIPTURE

Thou wilt shew me the path of life: in thy presence is fulness of joy; at thy right hand there are pleasures for evermore (Psalm 16:11).

WORD OF ENCOURAGEMENT

There are countless, wonderful attributes about the presence of God, and the Bible promises many benefits to those who experience it. There is joy, liberty, peace, and divine power in His presence. The Bible says the mountains literally melt like wax in the presence of the Lord (see Ps. 97:5); this means that nothing can withstand His presence. For the person who desires God's presence, it will destroy the demonic and also bring hope and deliverance. In our lives and homes, we must constantly pursue the things that invite the Lord's presence. Obviously, consistent prayer and time reading the Bible will bring His presence into manifestation. Attending church is also a key way to experience the presence of the Lord as you are surrounded by other believers in the atmosphere of worship. And lastly, tell the Lord how much you want His presence in your life and family! He wants to hear you express your desire for Him. Developing a daily consciousness of the Lord's presence will cause you to experience His overwhelming presence in your life, in your home, and upon your family.

ANGELS
SURROUND US

DECLARATION

TODAY we decree that the angels of the Lord surround our home and family. They stand watch to ensure that we experience no tragedy or harm. We prophesy that we are under the charge of the royal guard of the hosts of heaven. They are keeping us safe and secure. We speak that no member in our family can be hurt or injured in any way because of the presence of angels. We also say that they stand watch around the perimeter of our home and around every piece of property that we own. No thief, attacker, burglar, or plunderer can access our dwelling because the angels of the Lord are on duty and fighting on our behalf. The angels stand as ministers for us as the children of the Most High. Because heaven's ministering servants are at work, we can live in peace and complete security. Our family is surrounded by His angels!

SCRIPTURE

For he shall give his angels charge over thee, to keep thee in all thy ways. They shall bear thee up in their hands, lest thou dash thy foot against a stone (Psalm 91:11-12).

WORD OF ENCOURAGEMENT

One of the most comforting truths and promises of Scripture is the knowledge that the Lord's angels are surrounding His people. Realizing that angels are on duty around you and around your children and property is important. If we truly understood the role of angels, it would encourage us not to speak from fear or speak negatively. Sometimes we speak wrongly because we forget that not only is God at work in our situation, but He has commissioned angels to work for us. In fact, the Bible says they are ministers specifically for God's children (see Heb. 1:14). We must also remember that angels respond to God's Word (see Ps. 103:20). That's why speaking negatively can hinder the work of angels. We want the angels to respond to God's Word coming from our mouth. We don't want to hinder them because we are speaking words of fear or unbelief. Reminding yourself each day about the presence and work of angels around you will bring comfort. It will cause you to be assured that not only you, but each member of your family, will be safe and secure because they are surrounded by His angels!

NO FEAR HERE!

DECLARATION

WE decree that our family is free from all forms of fear. We prophesy that fear has no place in our home or upon any member of our family. We command all evil spirits of fear to leave, in the Name of Jesus! We declare that *all forms* of fear must also go. We break the power of worry, anxiety, fretfulness, insecurity, panic, dread, and terror. Our household is off-limits to fear. We refuse to give in or submit to fear, and we prophesy that we are a family who chooses to stand up in faith in every situation. We are free from fear because the Lord is helping us and giving us His strength. We have no fear of man, for the Lord is our help and refuge. The Lord is our light and our salvation, and we have no need to be afraid. We declare fear is replaced with faith and confidence. All forms of fear are reversed and replaced with assurance, calm, cheer, and peace. We are fear-free, in Jesus' Name!

SCRIPTURE

Fear thou not; for I am with thee: be not dismayed; for I am thy God: I will strengthen thee; yea, I will help thee; yea, I will uphold thee with the right hand of my righteousness (Isaiah 41:10).

WORD OF ENCOURAGEMENT

If there is one encouragement Scripture repeats again and again, it's the encouragement not to fear. Consider how many times the Lord or His angels gave His people the admonition, "Fear not!" What we can glean from this is that it's tempting to fall into fear. If we're not careful, we can look at the circumstances in the world or in our own lives and let fear creep in. We must resist the temptation to fear because fear is a debilitating enemy. It can paralyze you from normal life, prevent you from carrying out your purpose, and keep you imprisoned—both physically and emotionally. We counter the enemy of fear with the Word of God. Have ready in your arsenal a list of verses that serve as a continual reminder of why you need not live in fear.

When fear tries to arise, resist it and verbally command it to leave, in the authority of Jesus' Name. Don't dwell on fearful thoughts or they will escalate. Don't allow it to stay for a single moment! Resist it immediately and command every fearful thought to leave your mind. Declare every single day, "There is no fear here!"

REBELLION
IS BROKEN!

DECLARATION

WE decree that all rebellion is broken from our home and family. We prophesy that every member of our household has a heart that is flexible and reasonable. The hearts of our family members are submitted to God and surrendered to His ways. We break the power of any evil spirit that would draw anyone's heart away from the Lord, and we declare that all stubbornness, perverseness, and hardhearted or stiff-necked resistance is broken from our family, in the Name of Jesus! We command unreasonable attitudes and hardheaded philosophies to dispel and be destroyed. We break the power of any mind-binding spirit of witchcraft and command it to leave our home, in Jesus' Name! We say that every member of our family is open to God, teachable, and willing to humble themselves under the Lord's mighty hand. We declare every member of our family and household is softhearted and receptive to Jesus and His Word and considerate of one another. Rebellion is broken and it has no place in our home, in Jesus' Name!

SCRIPTURE

"What sorrow awaits my rebellious children," says the Lord. "You make plans that are contrary to mine. You make alliances not directed by my Spirit, thus piling up your sins" (Isaiah 30:1 NLT).

WORD OF ENCOURAGEMENT

The scripture here references Israel and their alliances with ungodly nations and people. Their stiff-necked ways eventually kept them from entering into God's promises. The lesson to be learned is that if we allow our hearts to drift from the Lord, we eventually find ourselves aligned with the world. Typically, when speaking of rebellion, we think of teenagers or loved ones who have strayed from the Lord and the hardship it places on a family. If you have a family member in this situation, then this declaration is certainly for you! However, also consider that we need to constantly remind ourselves to steer clear of all forms of rebellion. Some forms of rebellion do not mean one has turned their back entirely on the Lord. Sometimes it's a matter of disobeying something you know the Lord has told you. We must put up a shield against stubborn rebellion, keeping our heart soft and open to the Lord and each other. Command rebellion to be broken off of your home and every family member!

EMOTIONAL
FULFILLMENT AND WHOLENESS

DECLARATION

WE declare that we are a family who lives emotionally whole and fulfilled. We are of a household where our emotional state of mind is sound, composed, and secure. We keep our thoughts collected and our minds in control. We decree that we walk in mental stability. We speak to any broken or wounded emotions and command them to be made whole, in the Name of Jesus! We do not walk in any form of broken-heartedness and we declare that we experience emotional fulfillment and delight. Our heart's desires and longings are dependent on God, and we rely on Him to be our source of contentment. We prophesy that we express ourselves emotionally to others in a healthy and godly way. We say that all emotional outbursts or flare-ups will not be expressed in our home. We command our thoughts and emotions to come under subjection to Christ, and we say that we are emotionally fulfilled and whole!

SCRIPTURE

He heals the brokenhearted and binds up their wounds (Psalm 147:3 NIV).

WORD OF ENCOURAGEMENT

Out-of-control emotions are a source of problems for many families. A lot of things can affect emotions. Everything from life experiences to physical and mental exhaustion and even hormonal imbalances can have a tremendous impact on how we respond to life and other people. The key is to recognize the power of emotions and direct them correctly. Remember, God has emotions and He's given them to us in order for us to experience the joy and color of life. Emotions are not meant to control us or inflict pain on others. They should never be used in an ungodly or unbiblical way. Unless our emotions are submitted to God's Word, they can easily control us and determine decisions.

God's promise to us is that He heals emotional wounds and brokenness. If you need this type of inner healing, declare it over your life and also speak it over your family. Then, determine before God that your emotions and feelings will not control you and that your household will be a place where everyone lives emotionally fulfilled and whole!

GENERATIONAL CURSES BOUND!

DECLARATION

W E decree that all generational curses are bound and eradicated from our family. We prophesy that the sins of prior generations are broken and no longer influence our bloodline. We declare that all ideas, habits, patterns, and practices that are not of God are unable to operate in our family line. We break the power of any prior curses spoken through the spirit of witchcraft, and we prophesy that these curses are severed and shredded, in the Name of Jesus! As a family, we practice habits and routines that are the opposite of the curse. We live and operate according to the will of God and His Word. We make it our intention to look for ways to increase the blessing upon our family and in our home. We declare that going forward, we step into a new and fresh generational blessing that shall be manifest upon our bloodline, both now and in the future. We declare that we are richly blessed because the curse upon our generation is broken, in Jesus' Name!

SCRIPTURE

May the Lord richly bless both you and your children (Psalm 115:14 NLT).

WORD OF ENCOURAGEMENT

People talk about generational curses because they recognize the fact that many habits, strongholds, and sins are passed down from generation to generation. The Bible reveals that under the Old Testament, God will hold the responsibility of people's sins upon their children even to the third and fourth generations (see Exod. 20:5). This isn't because God is unjust and makes our children pay for our wrongs. It is revealing that what we choose to do today, our children will often repeat, and therefore they will end up paying the price for those choices. The good news is, generational patterns or "curses" can be broken! The Bible says Jesus was made the curse for us (see Gal. 3:13). He took the curse upon Himself so we don't have to bear it. In Christ, we have the ability to break the power of generational patterns, first by repenting of our own sins, then asking God to help us not to repeat the bad habits or patterns of generations before us. Then lastly, we can command the power of any evil spirits influencing these patterns to be broken, in the Name of Jesus! Declare today your family is free from the generational curse and God's rich blessing is upon you and your children!

SPECIAL MEMORIES

DECLARATION

W E decree that our family experiences special memories together that we will cherish for decades to come. We prophesy a closeness that enables us to cling to and appreciate every moment we share. We prophesy that no endeavor by the enemy shall be able to shatter our family memories, in Jesus' Name. We declare that we recollect the good times over the challenges. We reject any memories in our family that would draw our attention to anything that God wants us to forget and put behind us. We decree that any memories that have arisen from the enemy are covered in the blood of Jesus and removed from the archives of our minds. We recall and rehearse the laughter, joys, good times, and triumphs, and we ponder all these moments in our hearts. We say that our minds think upon the good things and upon the strengths, good qualities, and abilities in each other. We are thankful for each memory we share as a family, and we decree they shall remain valuable, special, and be passed down to our children and grandchildren!

SCRIPTURE

But Mary kept all these things in her heart and thought about them often (Luke 2:19 NLT).

WORD OF ENCOURAGEMENT

The Bible gives us a glimpse into a special family memory when Mary learned she was to give birth to the Messiah. After hearing the news, she thought about it on a regular basis. Undoubtedly, rehearsing what was happening would surely help mold and shape her relationship with the son she was preparing to raise into adulthood. Cherishing the memories of our family and loved ones is key to building a strong family bond. It strengthens us as individuals and also strengthens our relationships. It helps us when we remember the good moments we share, rather than highlighting the challenging moments or shortcomings we see in one another. Building memories is an important element to having a healthy family, and it's a key element in keeping families together. I believe the Lord wants us to be like Mary and think often of the good things in our family relationships. Laughing together and doing things together that will make us smile for years to come will cause our families to thrive.

IDEAS THAT PROSPER

DECLARATION

WE declare that we receive good ideas that prosper and excel. Our family receives concepts that come from divinely inspired imaginations. We receive creative ability from the Lord who causes us to become skilled craftsmen, entrepreneurs, and inventors. We declare that we dispel any creative ideas that are built on fruitless ambition. Nothing we imagine and design shall end up as a waste of time and resources, in Jesus' Name. We declare that we will never follow the path of innovations built upon man-made ideologies and fleshly concepts. We speak that our innovations prosper and evolve into revenue that shall be a blessing to the Kingdom of God. We prophesy new inventions and inspirations that come to us by the Holy Spirit. We declare everything we begin and develop shall be a benefit and blessing to others.

We credit our creativity to the Lord, and we command our ideas to prosper, in Jesus' Name!

SCRIPTURE

The Lord has given them special skills as engravers, designers, embroiderers in blue, purple, and scarlet thread on fine linen cloth, and weavers. They excel as craftsmen and as designers (Exodus 35:35 NLT).

WORD OF ENCOURAGEMENT

Most people have a desire to create. Whether it's some form of artistry, a business idea, or a type of service, people want to put their imaginations to work and create something amazing. Usually, the hope is that the creative idea will eventually bring about revenue. Unfortunately, we can all probably think of times when we had an idea that went nowhere. Whether it was the idea itself, a problem with our skill set or work ethic, or maybe a lack of finances, it's frustrating to attempt something and not have it work out. When families work on these ideas together, the entire family can experience disappointment. However, when we have confidence that our ideas are from the Holy Spirit, it empowers us to see them blossom. Begin to declare over yourself and your family that the things you design will be God inspired and that He will cause you to avoid things that are not of Him. Declare today that you and your family have ideas that prosper!

EXTENDED FAMILY
IS BLESSED

DECLARATION

W E decree that all our extended family members live in divine blessing. We prophesy that the Lord covers them with His hand and that they will be safe and sound. We speak peace over our brothers, sisters, aunts, uncles, parents, grandparents, cousins, and in-laws. We say that they are off-limits to the enemy and that our prayers over them bring a shield against the forces of darkness that would try to harm them, in Jesus' Name. We declare peace with all the relatives and that any disagreements, strife, offenses, or resentment shall be resolved. We declare strife is replaced by love, understanding, and grace. We decree that any extended family who are lost will become receptive to the Lord and be saved. We say that any family who are bound by any strongholds, sins, or bondages are delivered, in Jesus' Name. We call for the angels to encamp about our loved ones and decree that no harm, tragedy, evil, or calamity shall befall them. We declare peace and blessing on our extended family!

SCRIPTURE

For the sake of my brothers and my friends, I will now say, "May peace be within you" (Psalm 122:8 AMP).

WORD OF ENCOURAGEMENT

A lot of comical jokes and quips are made about extended family and in-laws. That's because it's often a place where problems arise! Many families are encumbered with a wide range of differences between households. And depending on how involved the issues have been or how close extended family members are, these differences can make life difficult. Sometimes the challenge arises from the fact that certain members of the family don't know the Lord and are against the things of God, while others are serving God. Sadly, some families are completely estranged from each other. All of the above can bring concern and stress. It's important to declare peace and blessing over family and extended family. Whether you are close or not, speaking the peace and blessing of the Lord, praying for their salvation and for offenses to be resolved, is important. It isn't right to allow these things to be ignored because we are carrying unforgiveness or we've simply given up on certain people. Pray for the peace of your extended family!

A NEIGHBORHOOD
OF PEACE AND SAFETY

DECLARATION

WE declare that the neighborhood where we live shall be safe and without disturbance. We prophesy peace over our neighborhood and over our streets. We say that our area shall be protected from violence, mischief, mayhem, accident, calamity, and destruction, in Jesus' Name! We say there shall be no robberies, break-ins, home invasions, kidnappings, murders, rapes, or any other forms of assault or acts of terror, in the Name of Jesus. We declare that all who live here live safely and securely. We speak over our neighborhood and decree it is a peaceful neighborhood that is calm and quiet. All who live here uphold a peaceful way of life that is considerate and mannerly, and those who would elicit evil will depart the area and not return. We prophesy the protection of the Lord is upon us and around us. We stand upon our sidewalks and streets and say this is a neighborhood of peace and safety and no acts of evil shall enter here!

SCRIPTURE

But whoever listens to me will live in safety and be at ease, without fear of harm (Proverbs 1:33 NIV).

WORD OF ENCOURAGEMENT

With increased levels of violence and unrest happening in the world, people are growing more concerned about their own safety. Speaking and decreeing the protection of the Lord not just over your life and home personally, but also over your neighbors and neighborhood is important. None of us wants to live in an environment invaded by some form of terror. I believe our neighbors, even if unsaved, can come under the Lord's protection simply because we are standing in the gap and setting up a hedge on their behalf. Through the power of our decree, we can become the restraining force against evil. We can become the "neighborhood watch," so to speak, in the spirit realm! We have authority over *all* demonic powers, and that includes those that would try to invade our neighborhoods. Your declaration over your area can be the very thing that will keep your neighborhood safe and free from the attacks of evil.

PROTECTION FROM STORMS

DECLARATION

W E decree that we are protected from storms and tempests created by unsettled weather patterns. We say that our lives, properties, and assets are off-limits to destruction of any kind. We speak to storms, winds, floods, and fires and we prophesy these cannot touch us or our home, in Jesus' Name. We speak in advance to all adverse weather and we say, "Peace, be still!" We are not fearful of the elements because we are people of assured and confident faith. Our family foundation is built upon the firm foundation of Jesus Christ, and therefore, we shall not sink or be brought to ruin when the winds and rain come. We shall always be calm and restful knowing all shall be well. We declare complete refuge over our lives from the power of all storms!

SCRIPTURE

And he arose, and rebuked the wind, and said unto the sea, Peace, be still. And the wind ceased, and there was a great calm. And he said unto them, Why are ye so fearful? how is it that ye have no faith? (Mark 4:39-40)

WORD OF ENCOURAGEMENT

In Mark chapter 4, when the disciples were in the boat, a great storm arose. They became terribly afraid that the ship was going to sink and they were going to die. Obviously, these were expert mariners, so for them to be afraid of this particular storm probably meant it was an unusually violent one. Naturally speaking, everything looked grim. But even with all the commotion, Jesus was sleeping. In the chaos of the moment, He continued to rest. In fact, the disciples had to go and wake Him up! The Bible tells us that Jesus got up from His rest and rebuked the storm and it ceased. We can glean many truths from this story, but two things stand out. First, Jesus was able to rest amidst the storm, which was by no means quiet. How could He do that? He was confident that everything would be fine because He lived in a place of steady, unshakable faith. Second, Jesus wondered why His disciples didn't also have the same assurance of faith. He expected them to be just as calm about the whole situation as He was. This is a lesson for us. We should be able to have faith and assurance that when storms arise, both naturally and spiritually, we can declare, "Peace, be still!"

ANXIETIES EASED

DECLARATION

WE declare that all anxieties or worries that would try to arise in our family are eased, in Jesus' Name. We prophesy that anything that would attempt to cause worry and alarm would be abated. We do not allow unnecessary panic, dread, or concern to grow inside our hearts and minds. We speak to nerves and tensions and we say, "Be relaxed and calmed!" We prophesy that we will not let our minds fixate on that which surrounds us, but rather focus upon the Lord and His unfailing Word. We say that the promises of God are manifest upon all circumstances and our family will not be shaken or shifted in our faith. We take all that concerns us before the Throne of God in prayer. We are thankful that the answer is being delivered to us from the Lord. Our family and household rests in the assured peace that causes our hearts to be at ease, in Jesus' Name!

SCRIPTURE

Do not be anxious about anything, but in every situation, by prayer and petition, with thanksgiving, present your requests to God. And the peace of God, which transcends all understanding, will guard your hearts and your minds in Christ Jesus (Philippians 4:6-7 NIV).

WORD OF ENCOURAGEMENT

When we face circumstances that cause us to feel anxious, we can become fixated on the situation until we are doing little else but fretting. The verse above begins with what sounds like a command. It says, "Do not be." Two things about this are important to see. Number one, the understood subject here is "you." *We* must decide not to be anxious. Second, it's not written as optional. With determination, we must *choose* not to worry, and then to that decision we need to add the element of prayer. We are to take our concerns to God in a tone of thankfulness. We can't come to God just complaining or expressing frustrations about what we are facing. We need to approach the Lord with a thankful heart despite the circumstances. When we do this, the Bible clearly promises that the peace of God will supernaturally take over. We don't have to understand how that works, but aren't you thankful that it does? God wants to ease all anxieties in your family today and replace them with His divine peace!

LOSS BECOMES RESTORATION

DECLARATION

WE decree that our family and household is restored from every setback and loss. We speak a divine restitution of everything that has been stolen from us by the hand of the enemy. We break the power of any patterns of depletion, deprivation, detriment, and disadvantage. We prophesy rebates, payments, reimbursements, and repairs. Every loss is restored with double and triple, in Jesus' Name. We declare that we live at an advantage and we experience excess and favor. We receive benefits and overflow that we don't expect, and what we receive in the future shall be far better than anything we've had in prior seasons. We declare over every member of our family that our minds are restored, our hearts and bodies are restored, and any sense of lost purpose is also restored. We command any and all losses to be restored and reestablished, in Jesus' mighty Name!

SCRIPTURE

God, your God, will restore everything you lost (Deuteronomy 30:3 MSG).

WORD OF ENCOURAGEMENT

Experiencing the loss of anything can have a detrimental effect on families and households. Whether it is a material loss or perhaps the loss of a relationship or loved one, God wants us to experience restoration. Of course, restoration is different from replacement. Some things that are lost cannot be simply *replaced* in the exact same package. Job didn't experience replacement when he lost everything, but God restored back to him twice what he'd previously had. Not only does God restore natural possessions, He restores your emotional state of mind that may have been deeply impacted by some form of loss. God will also restore our wellbeing from any trauma that we've experienced. God's character is such that He will *completely* restore! He not only restores physical possessions, but He restores the deep places that have been wounded. He restores broken relationships. There isn't a loss that we experience where God can't bring about a complete restoration that encompasses every element of what we need. If you are experiencing some sort of loss, declare restoration and allow God to masterfully bring it upon your household!

DREAMS BECOME REALITIES

DECLARATION

W E decree that all the dreams we have and share as a family shall be fulfilled. Our God-breathed heart's desires shall become visible realities before our eyes. Our hopes, desires, and aspirations shall not be delayed. We speak against the spirit of delay, deferral, suspension, cancellation, and postponement. We break the power of any demonic forces that would attempt to bring despair to our hearts through unfulfilled hopes and dreams, in Jesus' Name. We declare that we will not be lured into wishful ideas and longings that are not endorsed by God. Instead, we will put our sights upon dreams and desires that come from heaven. Our family will not experience any sense of hopelessness that comes from unfulfilled desires. We say that our dreams flourish and are achieved in all aspects, and nothing we hope for and desire will be aborted. Our family dreams become realities, in Jesus' Name!

SCRIPTURE

Hope deferred makes the heart sick, but a dream ful-
filled is a tree of life (Proverbs 13:12 NLT).

WORD OF ENCOURAGEMENT

Many people live a certain part of their lives wishing and hoping for things that at times seem unattainable. Some have dreams of accomplishing great things in their career; for others it's to get married someday, have children, or perhaps own their own home or car. For others, it's a little more far-reaching. They dream of just being healthy and able-bodied or overcoming some storm of life that is entirely out of their control. The Word of God reminds us that when our hopes and dreams are delayed, it can bring a certain measure of ailing to our hearts. The Lord wants us to realize that when our dreams become realities, it causes us to flourish in multiple areas. Begin to envision these things coming to pass! Sometimes our dreams are never realized because we can't see ourselves in a different set of circumstances. Begin to see and declare that every desire and dream in your life that is inspired by heaven will manifest and that you won't live day after day, year after year, in a state of hopelessness. Don't get stuck in the rut of seeing the same old things each day. Have a renewed confidence today that God wants your dreams and your family's dreams fulfilled!

BIRTHDAYS
OF BLESSING

DECLARATION

WE declare that birthdays in our family are great blessings. We say that every birthday celebrated by our family members is a time of rejoicing and appreciation. We say they are times of thankfulness unto the Lord. We prophesy that each birthday shall be filled with joy, gratitude, smiles, and laughter. We declare that no evil spirits of despondency shall hover over our family members on their birthdays, in the Name of Jesus. We declare grief and sorrow cannot invade us on the birthdays we remember of our loved ones who have passed on. We say that each person who is celebrating a birthday will feel surrounded by love, appreciation, and honor, and they shall have a renewed grasp on their God-given purpose in life. We say that family birthdays in our household are times of jubilee! We look for creative ways to celebrate each other's special day and say that each family member will feel the approval and esteem of God upon them. We decree that every birthday is blessed and there shall be many more to come, in Jesus' Name!

SCRIPTURE

You saw me before I was born. Every day of my life was recorded in your book. Every moment was laid out before a single day had passed (Psalm 139:16 NLT).

WORD OF ENCOURAGEMENT

Family birthdays should be special. They're a perfect time to show a little extra honor to the people you love most and to reflect on how God formed each of us. A birthday celebration is a great time to thank the Lord for our bright future that began to bloom the day we were born. Birthdays can even be a time to honor each other and set aside differences and hard feelings that sometimes arise in families. If we see them as special opportunities to reevaluate the areas that divide, we can move toward mending them.

Making it a point to declare blessings over family birthdays can have a tremendous spiritual and emotional impact and will impart value to your loved ones. God celebrates us and our birth, and so should we! In addition, if you can recall it, along with your natural birthday, celebrate and thank God for your spiritual rebirth. The day you gave your heart to the Lord and became born again is also a time to celebrate! Begin to declare birthdays of blessings!

ABOUNDING LOVE

DECLARATION

WE decree the abounding love of the heavenly Father resides in our home. Our family walks, talks, and acts according to the love of God. We are a family who extends love, even toward those who act and behave hatefully. Unselfish love governs all we do. We reject all behaviors, attitudes, and actions that are devoid of God's love. We command evil spirits of anger, hatred, unforgiveness, resentment, offenses, division, and strife to be bound from our family, in Jesus' Name! We release mercy, kindness, forgiveness, patience, and peace. We prophesy that abounding love is continually released in the atmosphere of our home. We decree that all fear is driven out by the perfect love of the Father. We declare that we have a fresh revelation and understanding of biblical love that transcends the world's idea of the meaning of love. We decree our family members are saturated in the love of God and abounding love reigns supreme upon us!

SCRIPTURE

But as touching brotherly love ye need not that I write unto you: for ye yourselves are taught of God to love one another (1 Thessalonians 4:9).

WORD OF ENCOURAGEMENT

Our culture clearly reveals that the world is devoid of true love. Often the world's idea of love is tainted by fleshly desires and selfishness. Other times, its meaning of love is to be accepting of anything someone wants to do, regardless of how sinful it might be. None of these exemplify the love of God. God's love does not express itself with selfish, sensual desires, but rather in service to others. Love puts its own needs second (see Phil. 2:4). God's love is also expressed through firm biblical truths regarding sin and morality. We are commanded to stand for truth and speak it in love (see Eph. 4:15). Now, while we are to be firm on where we stand, our actions, manners, and tone should all be loving. We *can* remain true to our beliefs and still be loving. Right now, our culture is saturated with unloving behaviors, and we must ensure our homes are places where the love of God reigns supreme. We must treat each other in a loving way; we must forgive and show kindness. Our primary goal must be for God's abounding love to flow through us as individuals and in our families!

ATMOSPHERE
OF LIFE!

DECLARATION

W E decree that our home is a place that celebrates life—it's saturated with the life of God Himself. We prophesy that there is an atmosphere of life upon our entire house and property. We say that anything that is opposite of life and blessing cannot operate here. We break the power of the spirit of death, decay, demise, and ruin, in Jesus' Name! We decree the curse cannot operate in our family or our home. We say that the curse is broken because Christ broke the curse for us and took the keys of death, hell, and the grave. We prophesy life, breath, longevity, health, and growth! We choose to speak life and do the things that promote life. We envision our family living and being infused with the divine, supernatural life that comes from God. We receive new breath from heaven, in Jesus' Name, and we declare our home is full of life. The power of death is broken and the atmosphere of life rests here!

SCRIPTURE

I call heaven and earth to record this day against you, that I have set before you life and death, blessing and cursing: therefore choose life, that both thou and thy seed may live (Deuteronomy 30:19).

WORD OF ENCOURAGEMENT

When the verse above uses the phrase, "I call heaven and earth to record this day against you," it is saying, today I have given you a choice, and heaven and earth are going to witness the choice you make. In other words, it will become obvious to you and to others whether or not you are choosing the things that promote life. Sin is a killer and will always result in death (see Rom. 6:23), but we can choose the opposite. We can choose life by making godly and right choices. We also choose life through the words we speak. Proverbs 18:21 tells us that death and life are in the power of our tongues. One of the subtle ways the enemy gets us to "choose" death is by what we say. Prophesy each day that there is an atmosphere of life in your home! Speak and declare that the divine life of God rests in your household and on your family members. Avoid speaking the things that promote death and decay. Avoid allowing the curse any access to your family because of what you speak over them. Make the decision to choose life and blessing today!

STRENGTH IN THE BATTLE

DECLARATION

WE decree that in every battle of life, we are strong in the Lord! We do not rely on our own strength or stamina. As a family unit, during times of trial we rise up in the power of the Lord's might. We put on the whole armor of God so that we may be able to stand in the evil day. We declare that we exchange our weakness for His strength because the Lord is our refuge in the time of trouble. We break the power of all weakness, timidity, fear, faintness, and fragility, in Jesus' Name! We prophesy that our hearts are not troubled, but we receive the comfort and undergirding of the Holy Spirit. We stand strong because the Lord is helping every member of our family and all is well! No battle before us is too hard for us to win because the Lord is with us and is holding us by the hand. We stand in supernatural victory that overcomes all the power of the enemy and we have strength in the battle!

SCRIPTURE

Finally, my brethren, be strong in the Lord, and in the power of his might (Ephesians 6:10).

WORD OF ENCOURAGEMENT

To receive the strength of the Lord during life's battles is truly a supernatural thing. But we must make the choice to consciously receive it. Otherwise, we will find ourselves fretting and, more than likely, we will make wrong choices. When we rely on our own strength, we often take matters into our own hands. We tend to do things after human wisdom rather than allowing God to guide us. Receiving the Lord's strength involves two primary things. First, we must speak it. Ask Him for strength and then thank Him for supplying it. Don't complain and talk about how over-whelmed and frustrated you are. Receive His strength by faith and speak accordingly. This will bring His supernatural strength upon you. Second, avoid making rash decisions out of fear or unnecessary urgency. Practice responding to difficulties in a calm, collected way and command your emotions to stay under control. Many believers miss receiving God's strength because rather than pause and trust that God has them by the hand, they act on impulse because of the pressure they feel. Ask God to strengthen you in the battle and then have peace today that He is undergirding you without fail!

EMOTIONAL WOUNDS ARE HEALED

DECLARATION

W E decree today that any and all emotional wounds within any member of our family are healed by the power of God. We receive the anointing that is upon Jesus our Lord, who came to heal the brokenhearted and liberate those who are bruised. We prophesy and say that any open internal wounds from past experiences, traumas, encounters, tragedies, or interactions are completely cleansed and mended by the healing balm of the Lord. We say pain from all toxic relationships is healed. In Jesus' Name, we come against any force of evil that would dig up past wounds, cause us to relive painful experiences, or encourage us to revisit old memories. We say, "Emotional wounds, be healed!" We declare no more bleeding, oozing, or infection. All is healed and alleviated by the anointing, and everything we do as a family will spring forth out of wholeness and soundness of being. We speak internal healing and health in our family, in Jesus' Name!

SCRIPTURE

The Spirit of the Lord is upon me, because he hath anointed me to preach the gospel to the poor; he hath sent me to heal the brokenhearted, to preach deliverance to the captives, and recovering of sight to the blind, to set at liberty them that are bruised (Luke 4:18).

WORD OF ENCOURAGEMENT

One of the key job descriptions Jesus used to announce His ministry in Luke 4:18 was an anointing to heal brokenhearted people. Countless people have been affected by brokenness from previous traumatic experiences. Often these internal wounds determine how we presently function and they affect our decisions and choices. Jesus wants every wound in our hearts and minds to be healed, and as a child of God you can receive His anointing for that! Also, demons will often attach themselves to these wounds and work to keep them open and bleeding, but Jesus came to liberate the captives. Not only does He heal internal wounds, but He will also deliver us from any demonic bondage attached to those wounds. Whether you or a loved one has suffered the trauma of emotional wounds and scars, know that the Lord's anointing will deliver and set you free. Declare over your family that emotional wounds are healed!

YOUR PROPERTY PRESERVED

DECLARATION

WE decree that our home is kept intact under the power of the Lord's divine preservation. We trust that the Lord Himself shall cause us to dwell safely in our home for as long as we desire to live here. We prophesy that decay, pests, infestations, mildew, storms, fires, or destruction cannot destroy our property, in Jesus' Name! We declare preservation rests upon our habitation. Even as the Lord preserved the possessions of the children of Israel, so shall the Lord preserve our possessions. We declare over our property: improvement, development, sustainability, security, and longevity. We dwell safely and in peace, knowing that the Lord will preserve us from all forms of evil. We declare our property is preserved and shall not rob us of our resources or our time. The hand of the Lord is upon our house and upon all properties we own, and we declare they are supernaturally preserved, in Jesus' Name!

SCRIPTURE

And my people shall dwell in a peaceable habitation, and in sure dwellings, and in quiet resting places (Isaiah 32:18).

WORD OF ENCOURAGEMENT

One of the things we often recall about the children of Israel and their deliverance from Egypt is that the Lord preserved their belongings. Their shoes and clothes were divinely preserved (see Deut. 29:5). It's important that we don't just see this as a one-time event. God has always shown throughout Scripture that He will preserve the properties and possessions of His people. Consider Psalm 121:7-8, which tells us that the Lord will preserve us from all evil when we come in and go out. This most assuredly includes the house we live in or the property we own! While it's okay to normally replace or remodel things, it's not acceptable to have things stolen or for them to disintegrate prematurely. Our homes should not be stricken with pests, breakages, or any similar issues. This is something that believers may not prioritize in their prayers of faith, yet it is something we do see in the Word of God. As a result, we know that preservation of our material possessions is something the Lord wants us to enjoy. Starting today, make the declaration that your property is divinely preserved!

A HOUSEHOLD
OF VICTORY!

DECLARATION

WE decree that our household lives in victory! We prophesy that we have a winning attitude and outlook. We see every member of our family as a winner, not as one who loses. We declare that the vocabulary of defeat does not cloud our discussions and conversations. We reject patterns and cycles of defeat and failure because our God always causes us to triumph! We break the power of collapse, setback, breakdown, and failure, in Jesus' Name! We bind the work of any evil spirits that would try to bring us to defeat and declare that we will not concede to them. We look at all challenges, trials, and opposition and say that we are well able to overcome! We prophesy that we are always above life's problems and not beneath them. We command the anointing for victory to come forth and reside in our household and upon us. We are winners in our health, finances, relationships, endeavors, business goals, and we win in our spiritual walk with the Lord. We do not slide backward, but we only go forward because the Lord has given us a household full of continuous victory!

SCRIPTURE

Now thanks be unto God, which always causeth us to triumph in Christ, and maketh manifest the savour of his knowledge by us in every place (2 Corinthians 2:14).

WORD OF ENCOURAGEMENT

Victorious living is one of the primary hallmarks of a believer. This is because we understand that the Lord is a warrior (see Exod. 15:3) and He never loses a battle. Therefore, if we are in relationship with Him through Jesus, then His victorious nature comes upon us. This means that no matter the problem, we can have faith and confidence that the Lord will bring us into victory. Notice the verse above says that God *always* causes us to triumph. It's not sometimes, but all times. If we believe that defeat is to be expected from time to time, we will find ourselves living defeated whenever we encounter a challenge. The Lord wants us to see ourselves overcoming and rising above. Even when circumstances seem beyond our control, God still enables us to stand victorious in ways that the world cannot understand. God wants your family and household to walk in complete victory today!

HABITS AND
STRONGHOLDS ARE BROKEN

DECLARATION

W E decree that any binding strongholds or bad habits within our family or household are being broken today by the power of God. We prophesy that all sin habits, laziness habits, or any lifestyle habits that prevent growth and success are being destroyed. In the Name of Jesus, we break the power of any addictions, patterns, cravings, hang-ups, or inclinations that are not from God! We say that we escape the power of all fleshly, carnal temptations through the enabling power of God upon us. Our household is free from all strongholds of satan. We release, upon our family, habits that form success and habits that are holy, edifying, and healthy. We have the strength and foresight to form the right habits, and we declare the Lord shall give us the ideas and the ability to walk these out. We prophesy that we are a family who is consistent and resolute in our objectives to develop God-pleasing patterns for living in blessing and abundance!

SCRIPTURE

There hath no temptation taken you but such as is common to man: but God is faithful, who will not suffer you to be tempted above that ye are able; but will with the temptation also make a way to escape, that ye may be able to bear it (1 Corinthians 10:13).

WORD OF ENCOURAGEMENT

"It's hard to teach an old dog new tricks." This famous saying means that once habits are formed, they're hard to break. The longer we do things a certain way, the harder it is to change. However, with dedication and a reliance on the Lord's help, we *can* change. Whether those habits are sin patterns, addictions, or simple routines that keep us from being successful in life, we can be empowered to break these cycles. Notice the verse above says that there isn't *any* temptation where God will not create an escape.

In other words, if we're committed to being free from the habits that hinder us, we will find that there is always a path to freedom. Deliverance is often found in making simple changes. Most of the time, trying to change too many things at once results in failure. Consider one or two things you can do and then add to them. And keep yourself immersed in the Word of God to build your faith! Declare today bad habits are broken, in Jesus' Name!

STRESS IS SETTLED

DECLARATION

WE decree that all manner of stress in our household is settled and calmed. We prophesy that our home is not a place of chaos and upheaval. We break the power of all pressure, strain, and tension, in Jesus' Name. We declare that all burden-causing issues that would weigh our family down must cease now. We command all situations that are invading our home to settle and come into divine order. We release relief, ease, and a sense of calm upon us and around us. We speak a sense of contentment and relaxation upon every member of our household, in the Name of Jesus. We say that we have wisdom and insight on how to prevent the things that trigger stress. We declare that no person in our family shall suffer from stress-related illness. We place all our cares and burdens over upon the Lord and we will not carry them in our minds any longer. We declare that all things creating stress are settled right now!

SCRIPTURE

Casting all your care upon him; for he careth for you
(1 Peter 5:7).

WORD OF ENCOURAGEMENT

The world spends countless dollars trying to alleviate stress. People are continually seeking out new ways to be relieved of it. This is probably due to the fact that life places greater demands on people than ever before. It is not necessary here to list out all the stress triggers around us each day. Stress is a monumental problem for many people and even causes life-threatening illnesses. Some things that cause stress are self-imposed, while others are things beyond our control. Either way, we need to do things that alleviate stress. In addition to countering stress by the things we do naturally through good practices and advice, we also counter the effects of stress by addressing the spiritual realm. It's important to recognize that demon powers are instigators of stress. They work to stir up the things that make you feel stressed and burdened. You can counter their attacks by learning the art of giving your problems over to God. Make a practice of declaring that you are casting your cares upon Him. It will cause you to remain conscious about not allowing stress to creep into your life. Then, declare that stress has no place in the life of your family members or in your house!

MARRIAGES ARE STRONG

DECLARATION

WE decree the strength of the Lord over marriages among God's people. In a day and age when marriage is under severe attack, we speak that a fresh anointing from heaven blows upon marriages. We decree that no member of our family shall suffer irreparable separation or divorce, in the Name of Jesus. We call upon the Lord to bring unity, peace, and wisdom to our marriage and to those of our extended family members. We break the power of all demonic forces that would stir up things to divide marriages, and we prophesy that no person, entity, or situation shall cause the marriages in our family to be severed. We say that all hardheartedness contributing to marital breakdown is softened and that hearts become repentant and pliable in the hand of the Lord. We release strength, love, renewed romance, communication, celebration, and joy into each marriage right now and we decree marriages are strong, in Jesus' Name!

SCRIPTURE

What therefore God hath joined together, let not man put asunder (Mark 10:9).

WORD OF ENCOURAGEMENT

If there is anything we need to pray and decree over today, it's marriages. The very meaning of marriage according to God's standards is under attack by the culture. Additionally, many people now view marriage in an irreverent manner; they don't take it seriously in the ways prior generations did. With so many marriages torn apart by divorce, many people now treat marriage carelessly and, as a result, the family structure has become compromised. Regardless of what the culture is telling us, we need to renew our thinking on how God views marriage and fight for the integrity of it. This includes our own personal marriages as well as those of our fellow believers and family members. Through the power of prophetic decree, we can release God's blessings on marriage. Make it your responsibility to pray for marriages in your church, among your family members, and for others you know. If you are married, fight for the integrity of your own marriage by releasing a decree over it and doing the things that preserve it. Stand today for marriage and declare marriages are strong, in Jesus' Name!

NO SICKNESS
IN OUR HOUSE!

DECLARATION

W E decree that all manner of sickness must go from our house—it's not allowed to reside here! Only health and healing are allowed in our home. In the authority of Jesus' Name, we reject illnesses, ailments, disorders, diseases, infirmities, syndromes, abnormal conditions, and afflictions. We command them to leave each member or our family immediately! We prophesy that no member of our family is unhealthy or sickly. Through the power of the blood of Jesus, we release healing, health, wholeness, wellness, new life, and vigor. We stand upon our covenant promises that healing is the children's bread and is available to every believer. We apply our faith to be healed and we do not fear the power of sickness or disease. We prophesy that no deathly illness shall arise or attempt to shorten the life span of any of our family members. We say only healing and wholeness rest upon us and there is no sickness in our house!

SCRIPTURE

And ye shall serve the Lord your God, and he shall bless thy bread, and thy water; and I will take sickness away from the midst of thee (Exodus 23:25).

WORD OF ENCOURAGEMENT

We should make it a regular thing to counter sickness and disease through the power of our words. It's a promise from the Lord that He will remove sickness from the house of those who serve Him. We need to stand firmly upon that. Also, remember that life and death are in the power of the tongue (see Prov. 18:21). We have the power to either release sickness or healing through what we say. Therefore, it's not wise to only speak healing just when you need to be healed. Speak and release it even when you feel healthy. This is important because it reminds us to practice healthy living and it conditions our minds toward health. When we do this, we are also releasing the promise of God into the atmosphere around us and reminding demon powers that we are off-limits to their attempts to bring sickness into our homes. We need to put up a standard against sickness and stand confidently upon God's promises for healing. Know beyond a shadow of a doubt today that God wants you well and declare that no sickness is allowed in your house!

GOD'S WILL
REIGNS SUPREME

DECLARATION

WE decree and prophesy that our family always lives and remains in the perfect will of God for our lives. We declare that in our home the will of God reigns supreme. Everything God directs and desires is what we will do. We say that our minds and hearts are committed to His will and purpose and not to our own. We reject any plan, purpose, or self-constructed pursuit that would deviate from His will for us. We come against any seducing spirit that would attempt to pull any of us out of God's plan, in the Name of Jesus. We declare that we will never miss the mark or direction of God. We speak and decree that each member of our household is attuned to what God is saying and is eager to adapt to His voice. Our declaration is that all our plans for the day, for the weeks ahead, and for the years to come are in the Lord's hands and we will follow Him.

SCRIPTURE

Wherefore be ye not unwise, but understanding what the will of the Lord is (Ephesians 5:17).

WORD OF ENCOURAGEMENT

Most believers will tell you that they want to be in the perfect will of God, but that can be easier said than done. God doesn't make His will hard to find, but there is a commitment to us finding it and an additional commitment to walking in obedience to it. But be encouraged! First, know that God's will is primarily found in the Bible. Regularly reading and knowing what the Word says will automatically point you in the direction of God's will. Even though the Bible may not tell you which house to buy, whom to marry, or what city to live in, it will guide you toward the things God endorses surrounding such matters. Second, spending time in prayer and praying in the Spirit will help set you on the right path to His will. We can't know the voice of His will if we do not spend time with Him. Finally, walking in His will involves *your* willingness. Make the decision in your own life and as a family that you are committed to following His will for you. Doing so will set your heart in the right place so that even when God may ask something you would prefer not to do, you will already be poised to obey Him. Declare that your family allows God's will to reign supreme in your lives!

DESTINIES
FULFILLED

DECLARATION

WE decree that the destiny and purpose for each of our family members shall be fulfilled. Everything the Lord has begun in us shall be completed and fully performed. We declare that no plot, plan, or scheme of the evil one shall be able to abort what God has started because we will not give the enemy access to do so, in the Name of Jesus. We close the door to anything that would cause us to abandon, neglect, or overlook God's purpose in us. We will never walk away from the Lord or become sidetracked by the snares of this world. We say that no member of our family will abort their divine and heavenly calling. We speak that we are a family who runs hard after God. We pursue His purpose; we will finish our race, complete the course, and keep the faith! Our destinies and callings will be fully realized, and we shall receive our reward from heaven both now and in eternity, in Jesus' Name!

SCRIPTURE

Being confident of this very thing, that he which hath begun a good work in you will perform it until the day of Jesus Christ (Philippians 1:6).

WORD OF ENCOURAGEMENT

We talk quite often about fulfilling our purpose in life. As people, we want to be able to look back one day knowing we accomplished what we believe we were born for. As Christians we take it a step further—we want to know we did what God created us for! Both are important because it's internally rewarding to know that you didn't waste time in life just going in circles and never making a difference—you used your talents, qualities, and gifts to the best of your ability. The scripture above reminds us that we can have confidence that God will perform the work He began in us. Of course, we must be committed to working with

God, but we can rest assured that if we keep pushing forward even when life presents setbacks and trials, the Lord will bring us to the finish line. This applies to our Christian walk and our task as believers to share the Gospel, but it also applies to the things we were individually put on this earth to accomplish. As you declare that your destiny will be fulfilled, you are building faith that nothing can interfere with that and everything you are called to do will be completed!

DIFFICULT PATHS
MADE SMOOTH

DECLARATION

WE decree that the difficult challenges facing our family right now become smooth. We prophesy that all paths before us that seem impossible to navigate are emptied of all demonic obstacles, in Jesus' Name. We declare the pathways are clear and we know which roads to follow. The Lord shall cause our feet to be as hinds' feet and we shall have the ability to move gracefully without falling or stumbling. We speak to every road before us and we say, "Be made smooth and easy, in Jesus' Name!" We say the Lord will lift us up and cause us to stand firmly so that we are able to maneuver through every place we are supposed to go. We prophesy that we have the clarity and wisdom to know how to walk the route ahead because our family is guided by the Lord's mighty hand. We will never say from our lips that we do not know what to do, for the Lord is always leading us and making the way. We declare where there seems to be no way, God makes the way! Our God is making the difficult paths smooth!

SCRIPTURE

I will go before thee, and make the crooked places straight: I will break in pieces the gates of brass, and cut in sunder the bars of iron (Isaiah 45:2).

WORD OF ENCOURAGEMENT

One of God's key promises is that He will smooth out the rough places in life that pose difficulty for His people. It's a promise we have to rely on in our hearts and minds every single day. Otherwise, we can look at the roads of life before us and a few of them might appear impossible to navigate. The enemy loves to present us with challenges that look unsolvable. But we have to trust God's promise that He will ensure that the pathway is made clear. It means God will not only remove obstacles that stand in our way, but He will also clarify the route we are to take in handling life's difficulties. This is especially important in families because as families we often make many decisions together as a household unit. When hardships arise, we face them and solve them together. If you and your family are facing a hard place, you can stand together knowing that the Lord will make the pathway smooth. He will ease the journey and make a way for you!

SORROW
MUST GO!

DECLARATION

WE decree that our hearts shall never be burdened and crushed by sorrow. We stand confident in God's promise that the Lord saves the brokenhearted and those who are weighed down with grief. We reject every spirit of grief and sorrow that would try to enter our minds and create a stronghold upon our emotions, in Jesus' Name! We prophesy that our family rises above all heaviness and oppression within our thoughts. We declare that we are lifted up by the Lord in every circumstance and situation and that joy and laughter always fill our being. Our home is surrounded by the Lord's grace, and we say that the atmosphere is bright and delightful at all times and nothing is allowed to cast a dark shadow of heaviness upon us! We declare grief and sorrow must go!

SCRIPTURE

The Lord is close to the brokenhearted; he rescues those whose spirits are crushed (Psalm 34:18 NLT).

WORD OF ENCOURAGEMENT

The world tells us that whenever we have gone through something traumatic or experienced some kind of loss, it's a natural thing to grieve. And while there is truth to this, we as believers are not to be under the power of grief in the same way the world might be. Through the Lord's grace and power, we can receive an anointing that will supernaturally help us to rise up from under grief and sorrow. It's one thing to experience natural grief for a period of time, but it's quite another to be overcome by a spirit of grief from the enemy. The devil wants to take our moments of natural grieving to an unhealthy level that would seek to bind and control us. How do we avoid this? We can only do it with the Lord's help. We must remind ourselves that the Lord has promised that He specifically stands close by us during times when we feel brokenhearted. He has also promised that He will rescue us from being crushed under the foot of anything that might cause us grief. Declare today that you are free from any spirits of grief and that the Lord is saving you from being crushed by any loss you've experienced. Our God is faithful!

UNDERSTANDING
AND COMPASSION FILL MY HOUSE

DECLARATION

WE decree that our home is a place where compassion is exemplified. We respond and react to everything through the eye of the Lord's compassion. We declare that every person who enters our home senses the care and love of God that discerns their needs. We prophesy that as a family, our hearts are filled with kindness, generosity, and consideration for others. In our home, we have hearts that understand one another's needs. We declare that we are saturated by the supernatural compassion of God that deeply moves us and results in miracles! We say that any attitude that is opposite of God's compassion has no place in our hearts. We reject any spirit that would cause us to become selfishly intolerant or inconsiderate. We say that understanding and compassion fill our home, our lives, and our family, in Jesus' Name!

SCRIPTURE

And Jesus went forth, and saw a great multitude, and was moved with compassion toward them, and he healed their sick (Matthew 14:14).

WORD OF ENCOURAGEMENT

When challenges in dealing with others arise, sometimes it's difficult to understand where another person is coming from. One of the hardest things to master is being able to put ourselves in someone else's shoes. It's probably one of the reasons people easily jump toward criticism rather than being able to pause and see someone else's position on things. Jesus, just after the beheading of John the Baptist in Matthew 14, was able to see the needs of the multitude. In the middle of His own sorrow following a deep loss, He discerned the need of the people. He was able to set His own needs aside and allow Himself to be governed by a compassion for those around Him. He didn't just muster up the compassion to minister to the people, either. The Bible says He was *moved* with compassion. This means, within Him was a deep yearning and care for what concerned them. And notice that His compassion resulted in miracles and healing! Compassion and healing go together. There is something special released in our home and family when we choose to be governed by the Lord's compassion!

FRUITFULNESS ABOUNDS

DECLARATION

WE decree that our lives are governed by fruitfulness. We say that all we do results in plenty, in flourishing, and reward. We commit ourselves as a household to bear much fruit for the Kingdom of God that we might be the Lord's proven and dependable disciples. We say that the grounds of our hearts are fertile and able to receive the seed of God's Word. We prophesy that we are able to avoid activities and endeavors that result in idleness and that are not worthwhile. We break the power of all barrenness that would try to prevent us from doing great things for the Lord. We reject wastefulness, infertility, emptiness, and desolation, in Jesus' Name. We say that our lives give honor and glory to the Lord so that those around us receive blessing from the fruit of our lives. We declare as a family that we have an abundance of proven fruit that ministers powerfully to others. We prophesy fruit that abounds!

SCRIPTURE

*Herein is my Father glorified, that ye bear much fruit;
so shall ye be my disciples* (John 15:8).

WORD OF ENCOURAGEMENT

Bearing fruit is the paramount requirement of the believer. It is what Jesus commanded of His disciples and what He also commands of us today. Christian fruitfulness should be cultivated with the express purpose of ministering to others and empowering them in the things of the Kingdom of God. As families and households, we should carry a culture of fruit bearing. This means we are committed to doing things for the Kingdom of God and working alongside other believers. The Lord does not want any of us to be idle, accomplishing little for the Kingdom. One of the greatest ways a Christian can bear fruit is through church involvement. Serving and helping in a church will help grow tremendous fruit in our lives. It enables us to interact with our fellow believers, work through challenges, and offer our gifts and talents. It also puts us in a position to serve others, and Jesus showed that servant-hood is highly connected to fruitfulness. Make it your goal as a household to become fruitful so that your family can experience the reward it brings!

ENEMIES HALTED

DECLARATION

WE decree that all attacks from the forces of darkness are being halted right now, in the Name of Jesus. We declare every demonic spirit bringing an assault against our family is bound, because no weapon formed against us can prosper. We say that every tongue raised up against us is being silenced by the power of God. We break the power of every liar, accuser, talebearer, gossip, and whisperer, and we prophesy that their words bear no fruit and fall to the ground, in Jesus' Name. We say that our family lives in a way that pleases the Lord and, therefore, it brings our foes to a place of peace. We say that we are able to shift our focus away from those who are against us and onto the Lord and those who are for us. We say our friends outweigh our adversaries because we have favor from the Lord. We call people in and around our lives who are supportive, helpful, friendly, and giving. We say that every enemy and attacker is halted, in Jesus' Name!

SCRIPTURE

When a man's ways please the Lord, he maketh even his enemies to be at peace with him (Proverbs 16:7).

WORD OF ENCOURAGEMENT

A person can have scores of friends, but when someone arises who acts as an enemy, it can consume you. Despite having many people in your life who love you, the negative effects of one unkind person can cause you to forget there are far more people for you than against you. When you feel attacked in some way, it is also hard to remember that evil spirits are driving the behavior of those mistreating you. Sometimes we want to lash out at those who are against us. While we do need wisdom and action to deal with such people, we also need to realize that simultaneously our war must be waged with the forces of darkness. Anytime we feel mistreated, we need to remember to command the demonic spirits involved to cease and desist in their attacks against us or our family members. Finally, the Bible promises that when our ways please God, He will deal with our adversaries. It's important to always do a heart check before the Lord and then trust that He will defend you. We need to learn to stay in faith on that promise and know the Lord will halt the works of our enemies!

TITHER'S RIGHTS!

DECLARATION

WE decree that because we are tithers, we receive the promise of Scripture that protects those who tithe and give offerings. As a household, we are committed to tithe and give into the Lord's work. Therefore, we claim tither's rights! That means no devourer, destroyer, waster, plunderer, or pillager can rob from us, in Jesus' Name. They cannot steal our blessing or fruitful harvest. They cannot steal from our home, business, or from any of our loved ones. The destroyer can't strip away our heritage or harm our children. We stand in the tither's blessing, which promises that the Lord will rebuke the evil one on our behalf. We stand in the tither's blessing that the Lord will open heaven's treasure and pour out blessings we do not have room to receive. We stand confident that the tithe is raising a standard against every demonic plot and attack. We have faith that as Jesus our Lord stands in heaven receiving our tithe, we are under the covenant of His blessing. We prophesy that the promise to the tither rests upon our family, in Jesus' Name!

SCRIPTURE

And I will rebuke the devourer for your sakes, and he shall not destroy the fruits of your ground; neither shall your vine cast her fruit before the time in the field, saith the Lord of hosts (Malachi 3:11).

WORD OF ENCOURAGEMENT

One of the most attacked doctrines of Scripture is the tithe. As one author put it, by nature most Christians are largely allergic to tithing! People often attack tithing because they don't want to part with ten percent of their income. Therefore, many excuses are made to avoid it. However, the one place where the Bible records that God Himself will rebuke the devourer for us is tithing. This incredible promise is something only a tither can claim rights to. It's foolish to excuse tithing by saying it's an Old Testament practice when Jesus our eternal priest still stands in heaven receiving tithes (see Heb. 7:8). Under the old covenant, people tithed to mortal priests, but we tithe to our eternal priest who stands forever! This makes tithing one of the most rewarding practices for a believer, and your family can claim the promises connected to it. You have tither's rights!

PRODIGALS
COMING HOME

DECLARATION

W E decree that prodigal, backslidden, and wayward children and family members are coming home. We prophesy that revelation from heaven comes upon them and they will make a sudden shift in their thinking and begin to turn to God in a supernatural way. We speak divine, heavenly revelation over them that causes them to miraculously change direction. We declare that the eyes of every one of our family members who have strayed away from the Lord are open to truth. We break the power of every deceiving, seducing spirit that is pulling them away, in Jesus' Name! We say the laborers are placed in their paths who will lead them toward truth. We prophesy that they have encounters and experiences that lead them to the Lord. We decree their hearts and minds are softened to truth and that all hard-heartedness is broken by the power and love of God. We say that any relationships, friendships, alliances, or soul ties that would hold them in bondage are broken, in Jesus' Name! We declare the prodigals are coming home!

SCRIPTURE

For this my son was dead, and is alive again; he was lost, and is found. And they began to be merry (Luke 15:24).

WORD OF ENCOURAGEMENT

There are few believers who haven't experienced the heartbreak that comes when a family member or loved one drifts away from the Lord. We feel this because a life without Jesus is one that eventually results in ruin, both now and in eternity. The consequences are high and, therefore, we have great joy and peace when our loved ones are serving the Lord. One of the most valuable things we can do for those who have gone wayward is pray. It's sometimes tempting to try and win them through constant pressuring. However, pressuring, nagging, and "preaching" can often make them more hardened. This doesn't mean we never present truth, because we do need to be sensitive to the Holy Spirit when He tells us to speak. What we can't do is continue speaking to them out of fear and frustration. When it comes to prodigals, we must use our faith. Our declaration for them during our times of prayer is very powerful. Things are moving that you may not necessarily see, but you can trust that God is at work and prodigals are coming home!

NO FEAR
OF THE FUTURE

DECLARATION

WE declare that, as a family, we have no fear or dread of what the future holds. We look forward to what lies ahead because we are confident that the Lord has a good plan for us. Our family does not base our view of the future on our past experiences. We base our view of the future on the Word of God and its promises! We declare that no negativity, bad experiences, or traumatic events can follow us into our future. We break the power of any tracking evil spirit that would use the negativity of the past to form our mindsets and beliefs, in Jesus' Name. We break the power of every form of fear and inhibition about what tomorrow holds. We are confident that the future of all our family members, loved ones, and descendants shall be protected and secured by the Lord's almighty hand. We prophesy that our future shall be bright, excellent, fulfilling, and marked by joyful experiences. Our family stands in assurance and faith that everything that lies ahead shall be carefully governed by the Lord and all shall be well for us. We decree we have no fear of the future, in Jesus' Name!

SCRIPTURE

Therefore do not worry about tomorrow, for tomorrow will worry about itself. Each day has enough trouble of its own (Matthew 6:34 NIV).

WORD OF ENCOURAGEMENT

With all the uncertainty in today's world, more people—including believers—are skeptical about tomorrow. However, we must remind ourselves that Jesus emphatically told us not to fret about tomorrow. He even said that today carries enough of its own challenges, so we certainly shouldn't be wringing our hands about something that hasn't happened! The problem with worrying about tomorrow is that it's a mirage of sorts. It's a concern over something that hasn't taken place, and by worrying about the future we simply borrow trouble unnecessarily. A famous philosopher once said, "My life has been filled with terrible misfortune, most of which never happened!" This is what worrying about the future is—expecting misfortunes that will probably not happen. We need to obey what Jesus taught and put the concerns about the future of our family, our children, and our lives aside. We must have faith about the future, not fear of the future!

PAINS
ARE RELIEVED

DECLARATION

WE decree that as a family, we are pain-free. We prophesy good health and wellness over our entire household. We say that our minds and bodies experience comfort and relief, not discomfort and injury. We break the power of pain, aches, irritations, misery, and physical distress of every kind, in the Name of Jesus. We declare that tenderness, soreness, throbbing, stinging, spasms, and weakness are alleviated by the power of the Lord. Whatever is out of alignment, disjointed, or malfunctioning, we command to be corrected immediately, in Jesus' Name. We stand on the promise that Jesus took upon Himself all our pains and, therefore, we do not have to bear them. We command pain to go now and never to return. We receive in our minds and bodies the Word of God that is health to all our flesh. God's Word goes into our bodies as medicine and causes every pain to be supernaturally relieved!

SCRIPTURE

But [in fact] He has borne our griefs, and He has carried our sorrows and pains; yet we [ignorantly] assumed that He was stricken, struck down by God and degraded and humiliated [by Him] (Isaiah 53:4 AMP).

WORD OF ENCOURAGEMENT

Make no mistake about it, God does *not* want us to live with pain. He doesn't want us suffering from emotional pain, but He also doesn't want us to suffer from physical pain. Whether you or a family member experience acute or chronic pain, it can take its toll on an entire household. The medical industry has discovered many medicinal ways to relieve pain because living in pain is debilitating. Consider that if natural doctors and medical professionals want to help relieve the pain of their patients, how much more would God, our loving heavenly Father, not want us to suffer from pain? Isaiah 53 tells us that Jesus bore our pains. If He bore them upon Himself, then we should have confidence that it's not God's will for us to bear them! We need to take that promise by faith and not go through life with various sorts of pain. Of course, part of being pain-free includes taking care of our bodies and doing things that promote wellness. Aside from this, we need to rely on God's covenant promises that He is the God who eradicates pain and relieves His children of it!

HOUSES AND LANDS ARE OURS!

DECLARATION

WE decree that our family receives houses and lands, properties and estates. We have given up possessions for the purposes of the Gospel, and therefore we receive one hundredfold in houses, lands, and possessions, according to the Word of God. We are able to be owners, not just renters. We declare no force of destruction can come against our properties. No fire, flood, shaking, wind, or storm can take from us or steal our family memories, in Jesus' Name. We also break the power of anything that would prevent us from receiving inheritances that belong to us. We prophesy that we receive benefits, assets, gains, and accounts. We shall never be without a place to live that is more than sufficient to meet our needs. Our home shall always be in good repair and pest-free. Everything we own shall always be in good working order. Our appliances, electronics, HVAC and electrical systems, plumbing, machinery, and all other equipment shall function correctly, and we will always have all of these things supplied. We decree houses and lands are ours, in Jesus' Name!

SCRIPTURE

And Jesus answered and said, Verily I say unto you, There is no man that hath left house, or brethren, or sisters, or father, or mother, or wife, or children, or lands, for my sake, and the gospel's, but he shall receive an hundredfold now in this time, houses, and brethren, and sisters, and mothers, and children, and lands, with persecutions; and in the world to come eternal life (Mark 10:29-30).

WORD OF ENCOURAGEMENT

We all know that life is more than earthly possessions. At the same time, life is meant to be stable and comfortable. Jesus came to give us life more abundantly, and a portion of that includes ownership of properties or a home.

The Bible makes it clear that when we make sacrifices for the Lord and His Kingdom, God will ensure we receive houses and lands in our present lifetime. As believers, we should have confidence that the Lord will always provide us a comfortable place to live and a secure living situation that has all its elements in working order. God does not want us living destitute, barely able to get by. God wants to bless us to be owners of houses and lands!

LONG LIFE IN OUR FAMILY

DECLARATION

WE decree that every member of our family and household shall live long upon this earth. We say that we live to a good old age in health and vitality and our lives shall be satisfied to the fullest. We prophesy quality of life. We break the power of premature and untimely death, death by disease, from accident, tragedy, or calamity, in Jesus' Name. We declare no act of terror shall come near anyone in our household in an attempt to shorten their life. We speak prolonged and expanded life and length of days upon us. We say that long life runs in our family line and rests upon our descendants. We decree that the day when any of our loved ones graduate to heaven, it shall be in peace and without struggle, pain, or illness. Our family members' transition into heaven in old age shall be without unnecessary delay and detention, in the Name of Jesus. We decree long life over our family, in Jesus' Name!

SCRIPTURE

With long life will I satisfy him, and shew him my salvation (Psalm 91:16).

WORD OF ENCOURAGEMENT

If there is any decree we need to be speaking, it is that of long life. It's a declaration one can speak their entire life that sets their future. It's a declaration based on God's promises to grant His people length of days. Premature death is from the enemy because it goes against the promise of Scripture. Of course, God wouldn't promise us long life if that life did not also include quality of life. God wants to give you a long, fulfilling life to enjoy! As believers, we need to not only be speaking long life, but also that our transition into heaven will be peaceful and without struggle in our old age. Sadly, some people's passing is lengthy and painful for not only them, but for their family. No one wants a loved one to suffer in their final days. We can begin decreeing against this in advance. The verse above not only says God will satisfy with long life, but He will show us

His salvation. The word *salvation* here is the Hebrew word *Yeshua,* which is the Hebrew name for Jesus! His Name is salvation! This points to the fact that as God grants us long, fulfilling life, we will also witness the saving power of Jesus at work throughout that life. Decree long life!

FULFILLMENT AND
CONTENTMENT IN MY HOUSE

DECLARATION

WE decree that we are a content family who lives fulfilled lives without want or need. Our attitudes are not needy, demanding, or unhappy. We are not covetous, envious, or lustful after material things. We don't covet the possessions of others or compare our lives with theirs. We reject the work of any evil spirit that would tempt us to complain, gripe, and grumble about what we don't have. We are grateful for all God has provided and given us, and we have thankful hearts. We encounter every situation in life with joy and appreciation and we continually envision ourselves having provision over lack. We say that our minds and hearts always dwell in peace because the Lord provides our household with plenty. We prophesy that we always have good things. We don't have to live with any manner of unrest because we know that good will always be provided to us as a family. We decree that each one of us lives with complete fulfillment and contentment in our lives, in Jesus' Name.

SCRIPTURE

Not that I was ever in need, for I have learned how to be content with whatever I have (Philippians 4:11 NLT).

WORD OF ENCOURAGEMENT

Provision is a promise of God woven throughout Scripture. God has shown that He doesn't just want His people blessed spiritually, but He also wants them blessed physically and naturally. That blessing includes having certain material possessions like a nice home, vehicles, and things to enjoy. In fact, the Scripture says the Lord gives us all things richly to enjoy (see 1 Tim. 6:17). We certainly shouldn't feel guilty about having nice things if the Lord has blessed us financially. At the same time, the Bible warns against covetousness and materialism that can cause a person to be dissatisfied with what they do have, no matter how nice it is. We are also taught in Scripture to appreciate what we already have and not covet the possessions of others. Being content with the things we have should be at the heart of every believer. A family that is content is a family that will live in fulfillment and blessing!

IMMUNE AND UNAFFECTED

DECLARATION

W E decree that we are immune to all the works of the enemy. Our family is unaffected by any plot, plan, scheme, or attempt of the enemy to bring harm. We declare that there is no method the enemy can use against our household. We live in the promise Jesus gave that we would tread upon demonic powers and stand in a place of authority over them. We declare that we shall always escape the snares of the evil one that would attempt to lie in wait and catch us by surprise. We are not fearful of any of the arrows or darts from the evil one because we know they cannot touch us. None of our family members shall suffer at the hand of the wicked one because his works have been defeated by the blood of Jesus! Satan cannot succeed against our family because we walk in spiritual immunity every day of our lives!

SCRIPTURE

Behold, I give unto you power to tread on serpents and scorpions, and over all the power of the enemy: and nothing shall by any means hurt you (Luke 10:19).

WORD OF ENCOURAGEMENT

There's an old saying that is sometimes used for encouraging people to take personal responsibility: "You can't blame it on the devil." This is mostly true, since we do need to take responsibility for our actions and, no, the devil can't force us to do anything. However, given the opportunity, he *can* and *will* apply pressure while attempting to launch a myriad of onslaughts against us. What we often fail to consider is that even though we are responsible for what we do, the enemy is often lurking about trying to entrap us or bring some form of attack. If we are not careful, we will blame ourselves and ignore the fact that satan must be dealt with through the authority Jesus has given us. Sometimes, we tolerate too much from the enemy because we think everything going on around us is our fault or responsibility.

We need to look more to the fact that there is an enemy on the loose and take authority over him by commanding his works to be rendered powerless! According to the verse above, there is no method the enemy can use to harm you. In effect, sometimes you *can* blame the devil and then take the stand against him that you are immune and unaffected by his attempts!

LAUGHTER LIKE MEDICINE

DECLARATION

WE decree that our household is filled with laughter. Our family always finds a reason to have joy, and we remain in a continual state of rejoicing. We prophesy that nothing can steal our gleeful hearts. We break the power of any evil spirit that would create sadness, sorrow, and moodiness, in Jesus' Name. We reject attitudes of cheerlessness, gloom, and hopelessness. We prophesy that laughter is continually in our mouth and it acts as medicine that permeates every part of our being. We say that our hearts are merry and we find humor, amusement, and gladness in everything. We declare that our home is filled with reasons to laugh and every person who enters shall be glad. We say that the spirit of laughter comes upon us, upon our friends, and all other guests who visit us. We declare their hearts shall be lifted and refreshed. We say the anointing of laughter from the Lord rests in our home and brings strength, healing, and wholeness. Laughter like medicine is released upon us, in Jesus' Name!

SCRIPTURE

A merry heart doeth good like a medicine: but a broken spirit drieth the bones (Proverbs 17:22).

WORD OF ENCOURAGEMENT

Laughter is something that even many health professionals recognize as having healing benefits. It has a good effect on the physical body, on our emotions, and even upon us spiritually. But having a merry heart that can laugh doesn't always come naturally or easily, and it can be easier for some people than others. Sometimes when difficultly presses upon you, there are times when you have to choose to be glad and maintain a tone of laughter about you. Sometimes you must laugh even when you don't see a reason. Even a manufactured laugh can escalate into legitimate laughter, changing a person's mental disposition in a matter of minutes. There is something laughter does that even the best medical intervention cannot—it releases a feeling of hope. Make laughter a part of your home. Look for the humor in everything, and whenever it seems hopelessness has crept in, let the Lord's laughter fill your mouth and act like a medicine to your family!

BLESSING UPON
OUR CHILDREN

DECLARATION

W E decree that the children in our family are blessed. We command a supernatural blessing upon all the children in our immediate family and upon those of our loved ones. We say that the generation of the upright comes under divine blessing and nothing shall interfere with it. We prophesy that our children are shielded against anything in the current culture that would try to persuade, entice, or influence them with anything opposed to the Word of God. We prophesy that our children and our children's children shall serve the Lord and not depart from Him. We break the power of any evil spirit that would attempt to harm, abuse, or afflict them, in the Name of Jesus. We say the angels of the Lord's royal guard shall stand watch over our children and destroy the power of any attacker. Our children walk in health, protection, prosperity, and security. We say that our children are a heritage from the Lord and they shall fulfill their divine purpose for their generation!

SCRIPTURE

Praise ye the Lord. Blessed is the man that feareth the Lord, that delighteth greatly in his commandments. His seed shall be mighty upon earth: the generation of the upright shall be blessed (Psalm 112:1-2).

WORD OF ENCOURAGEMENT

One thing that moves the heart of any parent or grand-parent is knowing that their children are blessed. Good parents want nothing more than for their children to turn out well. Therefore, we typically do all we can to ensure they are provided for, live in a secure environment, are given love, taught responsibility for living, and so on. As Christian parents, we also want to ensure their spiritual upbringing by teaching them God's Word, praying with them, and involving them in church. Yet another import-ant aspect that could be overlooked are the words and declarations we speak over our children. Like anything else in life, what we say affects our outcome. What we say over our children is a catalyst in determining their destiny. Getting in agreement with what God says about the children in your family is one of the greatest things you can do to ensure their future. Agree with God and decree that the generation of the upright is blessed!

BLESSED MIND
AND MEMORY

DECLARATION

WE decree that our family's minds and memories are blessed. We say that we are alert, sharp, and collected in our thoughts and perceptions. We break the power of all memory loss, dullness of thinking, mind fog, forgetfulness, or inattentiveness, in the Name of Jesus. We bind the power of all mental illnesses and disorders of any kind, and we say they have no power to operate in our family or loved ones. We prophesy that every member of our family stays on task without being easily distracted or disoriented. We stand upon the promise of Scripture that says we have the mind of Christ, because our minds are blessed in Him. We say all aspects of our minds function as they were created. Our mental will, intelligence, emotions, imagination, and memory all operate in perfect harmony and in submission to Almighty God. We declare that memory loss disorders have no place in our family. We shall live our entire lives fully cognizant and mentally engaged because we have a blessed mind and memory!

SCRIPTURE

For who hath known the mind of the Lord, that he may instruct him? but we have the mind of Christ (1 Corinthians 2:16).

WORD OF ENCOURAGEMENT

We often make jokes about forgetfulness, but in reality, memory loss and mental decline are no laughing matter. This challenge has brought sorrow to many families and is something we must decree against. The Bible makes it clear that we have the mind of Christ. While this verse in context is saying that we hold the same mindset or position on spiritual matters as Christ, we also know that we can't hold those mindsets without our mind being healthily engaged. The Lord gave us our mind so we can function effectively, and like any other health issue, we can stand in faith for our mental health. Avoid making jests about being forgetful or being "in a fog." Begin declaring that your mind is alert and engaged. There are many people in their latter years of life who are just as mentally alert as they were in their teens. If it can happen for them, then don't believe for less in your life! Stand on the promise of God that your mind is blessed by Him and nothing will take that from you or your family!

ABOUT
BRENDA KUNNEMAN

BRENDA KUNNEMAN pastors Lord of Hosts Church in Omaha, Nebraska with her husband, Hank. She is a writer and teacher who ministers nationally and internationally, seeing lives change through the prophetic word and ministry in the Holy Spirit coupled with a balanced, relevant message. Together, she and her husband also host a weekly TV program, *New Level with Hank and Brenda*, on Daystar Television Network.

$\dfrac{191}{96}$

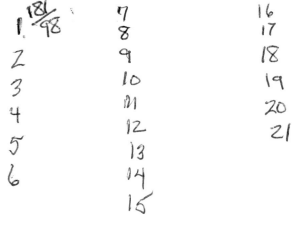

DESTINY IMAGE BOOKS
BY BRENDA KUNNEMAN

The Daily Prophecy

The Roadmap to Divine Direction

Decoding Hell's Propaganda

The Daily Decree